THE CHRISTIAN HANDBOOK ON AGING

Howard A. Eyrich, D.Min.
&
Judy A. Dabler

All Scripture is the author's update of the King James Version of The Holy Bible.

Additional copies are available. For your convenience, an order form can be found at the back of this book.

Library of Congress Catalog Card Number: 96-96883

ISBN 1-57502-284-2

Printed in the USA by

Morris Publishing

3212 E. Hwy 30
Kearney, NE 68847
800-650-7888

CONTENTS

PREFACE

This book has taken shape in the forge of life. Having grown up in a family in which the majority of my relatives were 50 years of age by my 10th birthday gave me an early introduction to gerontology. The intensity of my experience was multiplied when my parents became part of my household and my father developed Alzheimer's disease.

After my parents' death, I enrolled at the University of Georgia to pursue graduate work in gerontology. This academic exposure, coupled with previous theological studies, enabled me to develop a structured understanding of my own life experience. This book results from my experiences. All the characters in this book, other than myself and my family, are fictional representations of real people.

I pray that many will profit from what the Lord has taught me both in the institution of life and the institutions of academia.

DEDICATION

This book cannot be dedicated to any one person. In fact, some who deserve credit I do not know. There were many who assisted in making my year of study at the University of Georgia possible. My encouragers, while dealing with my father's situation and completing the academic studies, were legion. But my good friends and colleagues, Rev. Cecil Brooks and Dr. Charles Dunahoo, have been the facilitators who have enabled me to achieve the goal of bringing to print this project. I am grateful to our God for the role they have played in this process.

A WORD TO THE READER

This book was written with a dual purpose. You may pick it off the shelf, read it, and find it a complete unit. You may also use it as a Sunday School Quarterly, or in any other group study. A teacher's manual, under the title *Did A Good God Make Old Age?*, is available from Christian Education and Publications of the PCA, (800) 283-1357. It includes teaching aids, lesson plans, and resource suggestions for the teacher. A video by the author, which introduces the study and forms the first lesson, is also available. This material was developed for use in a Sunday School class, Bible study or small group.

Many older adults will read this book who are not involved in a study group where the issues addressed here are discussed. With this in mind, I found it pertinent to add Chapter 13.

When I decided to review and update this book, I discussed it with Mrs. Judy Dabler. Judy had been my student at Covenant Theological Seminary, and I had been impressed with her spiritual commitment, her intuitive spirit, and her research skills. Judy agreed to assist me with this project. However, when she brought in the research for adding Chapters 14 through 16, I did not have time to complete the writing. I made the decision at that point to invite her to write these chapters and to include her as my co-author. Judy also prepared the manuscript and added the graphics.

You will be hearing more from Judy as she makes further contributions to the literature.

1

DID A GOOD GOD MAKE OLD AGE?
Biblical Insights on Aging

"Let me tell you about my favorite school teacher," Tom said at dinner with several colleagues at a conference on aging.

"Susan Mayhill, Miss Susan as all us kids called her while growing up, never moved after her fiancé was killed in World War II. She taught seventh grade English when I thought being a seventh grader was grown up. Years later when my son reached the seventh grade, Miss Susan faithfully continued to press the round pegs of the parts of speech into the square heads of seventh grade boys. When teacher conference time arrived, I was horrified at the devastating effects which `Father Time' and crippling arthritis had inflicted on this once attractive, vibrant lady. In spite of her physical condition, I was overwhelmed by her sweet enthusiastic spirit, her mental agility and her genuine concern for her students. As I left school I passed the school principal in the hall and asked if Miss Susan had not reached retirement age.

"`Oh, yes,' replied Mr. Smith, `but she chooses to teach for personal and economic reasons. Since she is still the best English teacher I have, I extend her retirement grace period on a yearly basis. But next year, at age 72, I will not be able to do so.'

"Well, that was seven years ago. After her retirement my son and I decided to visit her regularly. We had learned that she had no living family and had exhausted her savings and home equity caring for two older sisters. We have watched this faithful servant of children languish in a nursing home. The arthritis has humped her over, enlarged her knuckles and knees, and limited her to a bed and a wheelchair.

"Often, my son and I visited her after church on Sundays. We had both left our visits disturbed. Only recently did my son voice the question which had agitated our souls: `Can God be good and be the God of old age?'"

Tom went on to speak about the spiritual struggle which he and his son encountered as a result of their love for the suffering Miss Susan.

This question had shocked Tom when his son had first articulated it. He and his family had been Christians for years. That God was good was unquestionable. They had often rejoiced in the goodness of God -- especially on their annual family vacations in the Colorado mountains. But, now, the accumulation of observed pain and the personal anguish of knowing the condition of their aged friend had triggered the expression of this forbidden question.

As Tom and his son drove home that day, they talked about the appropriateness of their question. Their inquiry led them in two directions. They affirmed the nature of God and quoted in unison the Confession, "God is a Spirit, infinite, eternal and unchangeable, in his being, wisdom, power, holiness, justice, goodness, and truth."

The second component of their conversation consisted of three questions about Miss Susan and her life.

1. What kind of person is Miss Susan?

2. What have these characteristics contributed to Miss Susan's life?

3. Has Miss Susan's economic plight been a blessing or a curse to her?

Their first question yielded a gold mine of Christian character traits -- dedicated, caring, serving, giving, concerned, enduring, and patient. She had truly been a saint. They decided that these character traits had brought her joy, satisfaction, and courage to face her pain; and, also that these traits had resulted from her close walk with the Lord.

As Tom told this story, he and his son had concluded that Miss Susan's economic circumstances had indeed been a blessing to her and others. Since she had to continue to work, she had remained occupied with others and not herself. Her personal satisfaction in serving endured. Furthermore, many students had profited from her unique ability to communicate. Even her years in the nursing home had afforded blessings to others, who like themselves, came away from visiting Miss Susan having received more than they had given.

"Her sweet spirit and joyful attitude," observed Tom, "made you forget her pain-racked body until you left her presence."

Tom and his son concluded that, while God may not have made old age, He certainly was the God of old age. However, they had determined to do a lot more thinking about the problems of growing old and the fact that God is a good God.

Where Did Old Age Come From Anyway?

In Genesis 3, we read about the fall of mankind in his representative head, Adam. The Lord God had given Adam great equipment. God endowed him with perfect knowledge to understand and live in his environment and to carry out God's assignment for him. God gave Adam great freedom -- the freedom to do as he pleased since he had a sinless nature and the power of contrary choice to remind him he was the created, not the Creator. God gave him a great warning: "You shall surely die." Adam made an irreversible mistake with eternal consequences. He died! Also, in Adam, his posterity died. Paul tells us, in no uncertain terms, that all mankind is dead (Ephesians 2:1-5; Romans 3:23; 5:12).

New students of the Bible often remark about the fact that Adam did not die when he disobeyed God. After all, didn't God come to the garden and talk with him? In fact, the Bible even says Adam lived to be 950 years old before he died. This observation appears correct. Yet, the fact remains that Adam died! His physical body began the winding down process, an aging process, which culminated in his physical death 900-plus years later. You see, old age is the product of sin.

While Bible scholars have some divergent views regarding the multiple hundreds-plus ages of those first people recorded in Scripture, the fact that the Bible records extraordinary life spans is not argued. The catastrophic event of the flood and the result of the aggregate decision to sin most likely accounts for the shortening of old age.

Genesis 4 through 9 records the corporate corruption of mankind. "Now the earth was corrupt. . . the earth was filled with violence" (Genesis 6:11). God's response to the corruption was Noah, his ark and the destruction of all flesh except those in the ark. In the process of the flood, there is good reason to believe that atmospheric conditions were permanently altered. Modern science has helped us to understand how this probable change resulting in much greater "exposure to the sun's rays" affects the aging process of our bodies. Immediately following the flood, we note a diminishing of life span in the genealogical tables and notations of biblical history. It appears that God graciously shortened man's opportunity to increase his propensity for sin. By the time we reach the life of Abraham in Genesis 12-25, 90 was considered old age and childbearing had long since ceased (Genesis 18:11-14).

Moses writes in Psalm 90:10: "For all our days have declined in your fury; We have finished our years like a sigh. As for the days of our lives, they contain seventy years. Or if due to strength, eighty years." By reason of medical science, mankind has been enabled to raise the average American's life span back to this biblical level of 70-80 years from 47.9 years in 1900.

Can God be good and be the God of old age? Four observations help to answer this question:

1. God did not arbitrarily impose old age upon mankind. Man was created to live, not to grow old and die.

2. Old age is the result of sin. Man was warned that he would die. Old age is the final phase of the journey towards death.

3. God seemingly shortened the life span in order to limit man's "refining of sin." If Genesis 6 through 9 is any indication of what we could expect from a society of sinners who live to be hundreds of years, God is indeed the God of old age who brings life to an end quickly.

4. God uses the limitations of old age to teach us who He is (Genesis 18:11-14). A good God uses old age as the final course in theology. It is our last opportunity to learn from our own weaknesses and frailty.

Overcoming Old Age

We all recognize that old age leads to death. If God is good, the question that haunts us becomes: "What has God done to counter old age?" If this question were raised in a small group Bible study, no doubt someone would suggest that God sent Jesus Christ into the world in part to counter old age. Someone may even refer the group to Genesis 3:15 as God's seminal promise of the Savior from the curse of death.

But, exactly what impact does the redemptive work of Christ have upon old age? In answer to this question, Christians learn a great theological truth which, if integrated into their thinking, will vitally affect their attitudes toward their own aging--even if the aging process is fraught with the difficulties of Miss Susan.[1]

The verb tenses of John 3:16 and John 3:36 also will enlighten you. Note that the first reads, "whoever. . . should not perish, but have everlasting life," and the second is like unto it, "He who believes in the Son of God has eternal life." These verses and others indicate clearly that eternal life is not a heavenly commodity to possess upon entrance into heaven. It is a present possession of the believer to invigorate life in time and space. As physical and spiritual life was destroyed in Adam's fall, so physical and spiritual life is infused at regeneration.

Seeing the Good God in Old Age

Christianity represents both a simple religion and an integrated, complex, theological, and philosophical system capable of answering the most sophisticated questions of life. We see the answer to the painful question, "Did a good God make old age?", in the simple faith of Miss Susan who believed that a good God loved her when her fiancé was killed, her economics depleted as she cared for her sisters, when her body became twisted with the pain of arthritis, and when she was relegated to a nursing home. For other, more questioning souls, you can determine the answer to the question of "Did a good God make old age?" once you complete a systematic study of the Scriptures. The antithesis of old age/death and eternal life exists for us all. We overcome the former in the present possession of eternal life. Should the Lord tarry, everyone will experience the aging process with the variety of attending hurts, pains, frustrations, and death. Thanks be to God, the war is won!

2

RETIREMENT:
Is It Biblical?

Mark will be 60 on his next birthday. At age 38, he formed his own accounting firm. He and Mary decided they both wanted to retire at age 60. Mark researched his situation carefully. He solicited several tentative lucrative accounts and concluded that he could attract at least three of them. He calculated that these accounts, in addition to the accounts he was servicing in his part-time activities, would give him a sufficient operating base. He determined that productivity for a 48-hour work week from April 16 to December 31 and a 60-hour work week from January 3 to April 15 would produce an adequate income to meet his goals. They agreed that Mary would serve as his administrative assistant and leave the office in time to be home when the children arrived home from school. Her summer hours would remain flexible, and the children would spend at least a month at camp.

He and Mary further agreed to two, two-week vacations, one in late April or early May for the two of them, and one in July or August with their three children. They also agreed to two three-day weekends a year for them as a couple, one of which would take place in early February. This would be their mid tax season break. They resolved to invest 20 percent of their income for retirement, to drive older, more economical automobiles, and to send the children to in-state universities.

They have worked well together and achieved their goals. They have even been able to buy and pay for a retirement home in Ft. Myers, Florida, where they have spent most of the family vacations. Mark is ecstatic at the prospect of fishing every day and walking the beach with Mary every morning and not ever having to be responsible to anyone again. They will have a very comfortable income of $40,000-$50,000 per year.

Jim and Jane, affectionately known as the J. J.'s by their peers at church, had the opportunity in their mid 30's to move to the West Coast where Jim would have become Vice-President of Sales for his company. One of the very attractive aspects of this promotion was the deferred income stock option annuity program given to corporate officers. However, after careful consideration, Jim and Jane turned down the promotion and accompanying benefits. They reasoned that the stability of their family, in the context of extended family, long-term friendships, and a balanced church life, were more valuable to them than the apparent secure future income. Another strong consideration concerned Jim's ability to control his business travel in his present position.

However, this opportunity did excite their thinking about retirement and precipitated some in-depth planning for Jim and Jane. During the next 20 years, they augmented future Social Security and pension benefits with a regular mutual fund investment program. They reasoned that this account would provide sufficient income to continue to provide at least the automobile which had always been company furnished.

At age 55, Jim and Jane both enrolled in a correspondence biblical education program which they completed by age 60. They also explained to their pastor their desire to become self-supporting church workers at retirement and requested an internship program "like the seminarians we have had here at the church." Between ages 60 and 62, they each served in appropriate positions under various pastoral staff.

They planned a trip to Israel, returning through Europe as their retirement celebration. The trip began with Easter weekend in Israel, followed by a cruise on the Mediterranean, and concluded with two days at the British Museum of Natural History in London. Jim and Jane returned to take up their new responsibilities as Minister of Assimilation and Assistant Director of Christian Education, respectively. Jim works 25-30 hours each week, while Jane works 20 hours per week.

Jim and Jane are now 72. Jane suffers from an arthritic knee, which limits her mobility. The church has run a phone line into their home and covers the expense. Jane continues her work, having shifted to responsibilities commensurate with her more limited physical circumstances. Jim has received what he considers to be his greatest honor in life. He was ordained under the exception clause (seminary education was waived) and officially called as an associate pastor of his church.

A Christian Understanding of Vocation

In order to think through whether or not retirement is biblical, we must start with an understanding of the nature of work. American society has, to a large degree, made work synonymous with vocation. We see this, for example, in the attitudes of many senior citizens toward volunteer work. Those enlisting senior citizens as volunteers find that seniors are not enthusiastic about non-remunerative work. Clearly, Americans think that one's vocation is one's paid labor. The American idea that remunerative work represents one's vocation and all other work is one's avocation generates confusion from a Christian perspective.

For the Christian, vocation refers to the manner in which you live your life. My vocation concerns living as a Christian. My avocation refers to my remunerative work. Then, the biblical conception of retirement would mean cessation from remunerative labor, not cessation from work. The American social conception so closely relates work and remuneration that ceasing to earn means ceasing to work. This convention practically influences people's thinking and behavior to various degrees, but the absences of large numbers of retired people from committed schedules of service in the church and other Christian institutions indicates that the American convention has become the standard of the Christian community.

A Biblical Precedent for Retirement

(Numbers 4:3, 30, 35, 43, 47; 8:23-26)

We do not know exactly how the American standard of

retirement at age 65 came about. A number of sociological, economic, and political forces converged to forge this present practice. These passages in Numbers provide several interesting and instructive concepts compatible with our American custom.

The first concept to note does not relate to retirement, but to entrance into the "professional" ministry. As you read these various verses and Chapters 4-8 in their entirety, we note that men were allowed to serve in the tabernacle beginning at age 25 and were enrolled on the service roster at age 30.[2] This assumes a period of preparation for life work, though certainly different from our own American preparation.

A second item to note in Numbers 8:23-26 engenders a discussion of the precise topic of this chapter. A biblical example of retirement is presented here. Some pastors might like to infer from this study that a clear basis exists for ministers to retire early. However, looking into these verses more carefully shows this idea of early retirement to be rather wishful thinking.

The Bible clearly gives us an undeniable example of God Himself establishing the concept of retirement. One could speculate upon the reasons for such a practice, but the Lord gives none. All we know is that an office bearer in the tabernacle service had to retire from his office and its professional responsibilities at age 50 (Numbers 8:25-26).

A third and very important fact also deserves mention here. These "retirees" had to assist their fellow workers in the meeting tent in keeping with the office, but did not have to discharge their regular duties. Therefore, we can conclude that retirement did not necessarily mean the complete cessation of work. These individuals continued to be active and productive people. They should also enjoy the prophecy of Psalm 92:10-15, which says in part, "The righteous man will flourish like the palm tree. . . . They will still yield fruit in old age."

What we see in this passage illustrates the example of God establishing retirement and providing the conceptual parameters for it. While you do not have to impose the exact age limitations of the model, we can still implement the principle that, while one may retire from his or her income producing role in life, he or she should still continue with an active and productive life of service for the kingdom of God.

The fourth commandment presents us with another passage of Scripture which impinges upon the discussion of retirement. The commandment says, "Six days you shall labor and do all your work" (Exodus 20:9).

Dr. Jay Adams has provided some enlightening comments on this commandment. He writes:

> ". . . The commandment does not require a person to be employed at the same task for the full length of his lifetime. Nor, indeed, does it even require him to be gainfully employed."[3]

What this fourth commandment does do is to call God's people to a regular routine (six days) of productive activity (labor) without age limitation.

In 1 Thessalonians, the Apostle Paul gives what I call Paul's proverb, "No work, no eat." Some of the Thessalonians had misconstrued Paul's teaching and concluded that, since Christ was coming back any day, then they would go ahead and "retire." Paul's instruction to these believers becomes sharp and to the point: If you don't work (provide for yourself), you are not to eat (depend upon others to provide for you).

"Well," someone will ask, "how can retirement be a biblical concept if I am to provide for myself?"

The answer to this question is quite logical. In America, the majority of workers provide for themselves during employment years through the deferred compensation system known as Social Security. Even though you may not agree with the system, in reality, it does provide compensation for the majority of workers. Social Security, coupled with various other deferred compensation plans, enable workers to cease employment and still continue to provide for themselves. Therefore, it is possible to retire and still fulfill God's mandate to meet the basic needs of self support.

Furthermore, this implies that, if I cannot provide for myself in a retirement mode, then I should not retire. However, Jesus, Paul, and James all make it clear that, when I cannot provide for myself, the church has a responsibility to assist me.

Looking back at our examples presented at the beginning of this chapter, we can see that Mark and Mary are not violating the Scriptures in terms of providing for themselves. They have wisely invested and planned for their lives so that they can provide for themselves. However, they may still be sidestepping some other biblical principles. Are they serving others? Are they using their gifts within the body of Christ? Are they regular in worship? Are they using their wealth for the kingdom? We need to address these important questions as well.

A man taught at a Christian university some years ago. He was like Mark. He had retired at 55, and went to Florida to "fish every day." In less than two years he realized that he was living an empty life. He then called the President of the university and asked if he had a place for him on the faculty. He said something like this: "I don't need an income, I need a purpose. The Lord has given me some excellent experience, and I've come to the conclusion that passing it on to young people to help them serve the Lord in business would be much more rewarding and God-honoring than fishing every day." This man built an outstanding business department at his university, greatly inspired his students, and became quite a contented man in the process.

In our final retirement example, we looked at the J. J.'s. The J. J.'s may seem like story book copy. You may even think that people really don't do such things. They accepted many new challenges in order to serve Christ in retirement and showed the qualities of conviction, self-control and commitment. Perhaps the J. J.'s appear to be the ideal characters of an idealistic author for one of two reasons. First, we find it hard to believe that anyone would elect to turn down the financial opportunities presented to them. Second, we do not expect people to transition into a new career when they finally reach retirement status. Perhaps our own expectations hinder us from pursuing and accepting these types of challenges as well.

Conclusion

Christian retirement refers to the cessation of regular remunerative employment for the purpose of sustenance. It does not mean the cessation of the expending of energy in productive activity. As Dr. Adams observes:

> "Work per se is not a curse from which we should look forward to being retired; it is a meaningful joy and privilege given by God in reflection of His own work of creation."[4]

Retirement, then, does not mean the cessation of work, but of employment (avocation). Work instead represents an intricate part of life. Retirement frees people from an employment routine to engage their energies in productive activities of their choice. What determines the Christian quality of retirement focuses upon what is done with one's time and energy.

Here are some questions for you to ponder regarding Mark and Mary and the J. J.'s.

In light of the biblical material considered in this chapter, answer the following questions by comparing and contrasting the couples in the opening vignettes:

1. How do you think each couple's peers would feel about them six months after retirement?

2. List the good values each couple manifested.

3. If you visited Mark and Mary after five years, what would you most likely expect to observe?

4. What did both couples do which should be instructive for us?

A Postscript

A Third Couple

John and Joan visit with their pastor and present the following facts to him. They desire his advice. John and Joan were married three days after graduation from high school. John has worked faithfully at the furniture manufacturing plant in town. He has served for 44 years as a warehouseman. Joan was a good mother to three fine girls who are now her friends. They take her out for lunch almost every Thursday.

Though finances always seemed tight, John and Joan decided that she would not enter the work force. Their three daughters went to the local state university, but for John and Joan the expenses still seemed high. Though health related expenses have been almost non-existent, John has not been able to save more than $2,000 or $3,000 at any one time. They face retirement in just 12 months, with a combined income from a pension and Social Security of about $1,155.00 a month, and a home paid in full. The taxes and insurance on their home amount to approximately $650.00 per year. Overall, they face about a $6,500.00 per year loss of income, with no decrease in expenses.

John and Joan have also been faithful Christians. They tithe, teach Sunday School, and both have served on various committees. They desire to increase these activities after John retires, but realize that they must also generate some additional income.

After listening to this data, Pastor Jones presented a number of ideas to them. They found themselves most excited when he suggested the possibility of their spending the summer working at the denomination's summer retreat. His proposal ran something like this:

"John, you could provide leadership for the maintenance staff, and Joan, you would make a perfect hostess in the dining room. The church could lease your home for the three summer months for $150.00 each month to provide housing for a summer intern couple. The retreat center would provide your housing for the summer and $1,500.00 each for your services. Eliminating your grocery costs, your utilities, and your auto expenses, and adding these savings to the potential income should drop your expected retirement deficit to about $2,000.00."

They were both very encouraged after their conversation with Pastor Jones. They then requested an interview with the retreat manager and indicated that they would gather the family together to pray about this opportunity.

We must also remember that retirement service or ministry is not limited strictly to the financially secure in American society. The Lord's people cross all barriers of society and education. All believers have a role in the body of Christ. The challenge for us is to be creative as we prayerfully consider how we can serve. Also, we must remember that the Lord provides for His own. A step of faith may seem just as appropriate for the retiree as it is for the young person who steps out trusting the Lord for finances, health, and the ability to carry out a ministry.

3

MYTHS, MYOPIA, AND MAYTAGS

Myths

One of the necessary components of understanding the aging of ourselves and others concerns the demythologization of our cultural folklore about "old people." Demythologization refers to a fancy way of saying that we must investigate current assumptions about aging in our society and compare them with the facts. Furthermore, it means that we must adjust our individual and collective behavior to the facts.

Myth One

Elderly people are nonproductive. A common belief is that the elderly neither desire to nor are capable of contributing productively to society. Undoubtedly, this myth has several roots. At least two of these roots society has planted and harvested.

Society arbitrarily established an age for retirement when the population bulged with young people who put pressure on the job market. The extension of longevity for the masses was not yet perceived as a problem. The retirees began to be viewed as people past this "magic age" of productivity. Of course, many did become non-productive. To be retired, early on, meant to be free not to work. Since productivity was measured in terms of economic contribution, elderly retirees thus became non-productive.

The establishment of a retirement age, followed by an expected unproductive, non-income producing period, contributed to the myth that elderly people are nonproductive.

The second root of this myth involves the standard by which we have measured older adults. In our fast-paced society, we measure older adults by the speed and vigor of youth. However, accuracy, depth of perception, reliability, and wisdom all represent valuable contributions to success. The older worker, while losing speed and vigor, brings the above qualities to the marketplace and contributes to the common goals of productivity.

A number of studies have verified that older workers are, in fact, perceptive, reliable, and wise. Furthermore, many dimensions to life exist beyond that of economic production. Frequently the elderly produce services which the young cannot because economic concerns may be less for the elderly.

Myth Two

Travel, leisure, and entertainment include the chief concerns for the elderly. Many believe that the elderly of the North anxiously await retirement so that they can move to Florida. Developers spend a lot of money advertising to persuade older Americans to accept this way of thinking.

However, Frank and Betty are typical of most retirees. At the age of 70, they work part-time jobs, serve in social organizations, and carry on an active church life in the community where they have lived for 40 years. Mary has learned how to operate a computer in order to manage the business affairs for a local Christian social service. Like Mary, there are many other elderly people busy learning so that they can take on new challenges.

These folks do enjoy more leisure. They travel more frequently, both for pleasure and family reasons, but their lives are full of rich rewarding service for the King and the Kingdom.

Myth Three

The learning ability of older adults has diminished. All of us can think of an example where this is true. But is it true because of age, or is it true because of a physiological problem with the individual? Researchers agree that, even though older adults learn less rapidly, they nonetheless learn effectively.

Believing this very myth could perhaps even impede the learning curve. Furthermore, believing this myth generates both fear and pride. Fear says, "I can't learn this." Pride says, "I can't learn this, so I'd better not try, or I'll look like a fool when I fail." Fear and pride are two things Christians are expected to deal with throughout life with their spiritual resources. Demythologizing the cultural myth that the learning ability of older adults has diminished may remove the temptation toward fear and pride. Christians have the resources to defeat the temptation, even if they believe the myth.

Myth Four

Older people do not have an interest in or a desire to be involved with people in other age groups. Society tends to group the elderly in accordance with the phases of the life cycle. Sunday School classes, social groups, and even prayer groups are broken down by age categories. We have a great need to make associations more age-integrated, as they once were during Bible times. At one time, grandparents, children, and grandchildren all lived under the same roof. With society designed after the "nuclear family," individuals frequently lack the understanding and love from other generations. There is a growing consensus that intergenerational interaction is vital to well-being. A practical experience in a pilot project with senior adults exploded this myth for me.

While developing a program for a large Presbyterian Church in America, we invited a girls' chorus from the local Christian high school to sing at the Christmas program. The chorus director suggested that her girls bring a sack lunch and join the senior adults for lunch. They agreed. They arranged the tables in a long "U," with the senior adults seated around the outside of the "U". The girls spread out and sat on the inside of the "U." Both the girls and the seniors talked for weeks about the joy of that fellowship. Senior adults need and desire intergenerational contacts. To believe otherwise is to believe a myth.

Myth Five

Older adults are physically weak. Of the frail elderly, those 85 and older, this myth approaches the truth. However, the vast majority of those 62 and over appear to be in reasonably good health. They enjoy a vigor that is reflected in a plethora of activities from golf to square dancing.

We also need to remember that physical strength is an individual matter. It directly results from health, exercise, diet, and mental attitude. While a gentle decline in intensity of strength which accompanies aging occurs, it certainly is a myth to attribute a general state of weakness to the older adult population.

Myth Six

Older adults are empty, uninteresting, and possess little worthwhile wisdom. I taught a newly formed "Single Again" Sunday School class which had no age parameters. Somewhat to my surprise, a 71 year old widow showed up in the class. I watched with great interest what response her presence would elicit from the mid-life divorcees, and I was pleasantly surprised. Apparently, these folks had not yet learned this cultural myth. We treated our senior member with respect and still welcomed her as "one with us."

Her initial response reflected that she may have believed this myth. During an icebreaker exercise in which she had to question her partner and then introduce this person with the information she had gained, she commented, "Well, I can't tell you a lot about her. I talked too much so she would know a lot about me. I figured she needed to know a lot so she could find something interesting to say."

As you read through these myths, it should become clear that the Christian, of all people, should not fall prey to these myths and this one in particular. The Christian has a responsibility to view our aging society in a manner which values each individual person. We must accept and appreciate individual differences. Each of these myths may be true of individuals, but they are myths when applied to the older population as a whole. Love, acceptance, and justice should serve as the hallmarks of the church. As believers in the

Scriptures, Christians cannot allow these myths to shape the way they view their own aging or the aging of others. Therefore, our theology must be ageless in its application, except in those areas where God speaks an age-endowed word.

Myopia

Susan: *Pastor, I'm becoming concerned for my mother. When Dad died ten years ago we were all amazed at how well she rebounded and adjusted to widowhood.*

Pastor: *How old was she then?*

Susan: *She was 52. Dad had truly been the head of the family, so Mom had to learn to do everything. And she did. She has handled her own financial affairs, kept her home in repair, planned several trips, and maintained an active social life.*

Pastor: *Sounds like a lady that you need not be too concerned about.*

Susan: *Well, I wasn't until about a year ago. Within about a month, she had some serious problems with her left eye and was diagnosed with diabetes. In addition, her good friend, also a widow, was mugged. Whether a result of these things or not, I don't know, but in the past ten months, Mother does not seem to be able to think of anyone but herself.*

Pastor: *Susan, could you be more specific?*

Susan: *Well, yes, I can. She talks about her smallest aches and pains like they were catastrophic. She relates them to the diabetes and speculates how severe they will become. She talks about how hard life will be when Social Security goes broke. You would have thought she* *owned millions in stocks the way she cried over "black Monday" when, in fact, the stocks give her less than a $1,000.00 per year income.*

When her refrigerator had to be repaired ($67) it generated weeks of speculation of what would be next. But, you see, Pastor, nothing has really changed. Life is no different now, except for a mild case of diabetes, than it has been for the last ten years. I'm concerned. Is she becoming senile?

Pastor: *The symptoms you have described do not sound like senility. I would suggest you run them by her doctor the next time you take her to his office and let him give you a medical opinion.*

Your mother is developing what I have come to call "Aging Myopia." Almost all people develop this problem to some extent at some point in the aging process. "Aging Myopia" means a personal near-sightedness. It refers to a preoccupation with oneself. The self becomes the focus of attention, both in the private world of thoughts and the public life of relationships. Self-concerns dominate conversations.

Sometimes an experience or cluster of experiences like your mother had will trigger this change of personality. What we would think of as a legitimate period of self-concern soon becomes a way of life. The individual begins to measure everything in terms of an exaggerated concern for himself or herself.

Susan: *But, Pastor, how do we change this?*

Pastor: *Let me suggest that you ask your mother to visit our counseling center. Pastor Jones is not only a skilled biblical counselor, but he is also a senior citizen who has experienced some physical difficulties himself. In spite of these problems, however, he has led the development of this ministry.*

"Aging myopia" usually results from one of two causes. The most common root cause is anxiety. Often, occasions for anxiety increase as we grow older. These may vary from health concerns to financial austerity. All of these anxiety triggers share a common root--a lack of trust in our sovereign God. Consider the two passages in Philippians 4:4-7 and Matthew 6:25-34 and ask the question, "Is there an age limitation on these commandments?" .

The second cause of "aging myopia" involves a lack of concern for others. The Lord tells us that to find our life we must lose it (Matthew 16:24-28). Rather than being self-centered, we are to be other-centered. When we become busy investing ourselves in ministry to others, we are wearing lenses that correct our aging myopia. When we look in the mirror of life through these lenses, our perspective on ourselves is accurate. The elderly person who would save his life must first lose it in service for Jesus.

A dear woman I knew as a boy growing up had every possible occasion to develop "aging myopia" early in life. She lost 7 children, she had surgery 13 times before age 50, and she experienced several other serious physical problems. Yet, this lady still managed to maintain an "other" orientation to life. Each year, after Christmas, she would begin to make the rounds of fabric stores where she would buy remnant material. From these materials, she would fashion 25-30 children's dresses, which she then wrapped and gave to the needy children at Christmas. At age 62, after her son went to college, she returned to a sewing factory and worked for 6 years to contribute to his education. Later, she went to live with him and his family. Because of severe hearing problems, she no longer attended church, however, each Sunday, her preacher son and his family returned home to a full course Sunday dinner.

This mother did not develop "aging myopia" because she kept investing herself in others, even though her world of others, the last ten years of her life, was restricted almost entirely to family.

Maytags

If you have never owned a Maytag washing machine, you probably do not appreciate their advertisements. Maytags are advertised as being so well built that they require very little repair service over their lifetime. A family with whom I spent much time in my earlier years owned a Maytag. When the oldest of 5 turned about 14, the washer finally had to have some rebuilding.

The Lord built most of us as "Maytags." Statistics tell us that only 5 percent of the aging population reside in nursing homes. Most people over 65, even if they experience a chronic health problem, still experience a well rounded lifestyle.

The analogy of the Maytag goes further than simply long life with little attention. The Maytag Company created their washers not just for long life, but for a long life of service. In much the same way, God created us for a long life of service.

Before retirement, most people work at least 40 hours per week. Some only work for a paycheck to enjoy the weekend. Others are much more concerned with providing for their families. However, at retirement, they entertain thoughts of full-time traveling, fishing and golfing. This type of retirement is like unplugging a perfectly good Maytag.

As you progress through this study, consider your retirement life in terms of the Creator's design. You will have opportunities along the way to help you make some evaluations. Options are suggested for consideration, and thoughts of a complacent retirement may be challenged.

4

AGING GRACEFULLY

A pastor friend approached a meeting of his church officers. He was running late, so the men had engaged in some lighthearted conversation while waiting for his arrival. As my friend stepped into the room, he noticed all heads turned toward the eldest member of the group who was in his early 70's. The gentleman's reply, "Don't look at me, fellows; it's not over yet," brought a chorus of good natured laughter. At that moment, they noted my friend's presence and a man said, "Oh, hello, Pastor. We had been discussing when the joys of marital intimacy ceases. You just heard Jack's answer."

Jack was aging gracefully. He retained a good sense of humor. It was refreshing how he could chuckle with the men and still talk about the intimacy of his personal life.

"I hate the idea of growing old," said 45-year-old Mary. "I refuse to let aging change me," she continued. "I am going to do everything I do that makes me "me" until the day I die." Mary's determination may be overstated and not sound very graceful, but her intention remains clear and she maintains a positive attitude.

Change is difficult, yet inevitable. Growing older gracefully depends upon how we process change. Our attitude results from how we have learned to think about the Lord, life, and living. Aging gracefully does not start at age 65 or 70. Rather, it is an integral function of our lives, particularly of our adult lives. The Apostle Paul said to the Philippians, "For me to live is Christ and to die is gain. . . to abide in the flesh is far more needful for you. . . and for your furtherance and joy of faith. . . ." Paul's attitude conveyed a realistic focus on the needs of others.

His attitude represents an attitude of continual growth and

service. Notice Paul's words in Philippians:

> "Fulfill ye my joy, that ye be like-minded, having the same love, being of one accord, of one mind. Let nothing be done through strife or vain glory, but in lowliness of mind let each esteem others better than themselves. Look not every man on his own things (only), but every man also on the things of others" (Philippians 2:2-4).

> ". . . work out your own salvation with fear and trembling. For it is God who worketh in you both to will and to do of his good pleasure. . . . Do all things without murmuring and disputing" (Philippians 2:12-14).

We have often perceived childhood and old age as victims of the same myth. We have also depicted each of these as a time of peace and serenity. Common observation and scientific studies both indicate otherwise, however. Gerontological studies reveal that older people experience more stress than any other age group. The loss of health, the death of a spouse, the crisis of retirement, and the empty nest are included within these categories of stress-triggering events. If you have not taken the time to cultivate a biblical attitude before the onset of these stressors, aging gracefully will prove to be a difficult task at best.

At age 56, James had to give up farming. He was not yet ready to retire, and his finances dictated that he must find another career. His wife, Martha, his junior by six years, decided to move to the city with their son to begin working on a college degree in art. James remained in the country to liquidate the farm business. Shortly after Martha's arrival to the city, doctors diagnosed their 36-year-old son with cancer. Six months later, James was told by doctors that he would permanently lose sight in his right eye within a year.

James accumulated more stress in one year than he had previously experienced in 25 years. All of these crises demanded change from James.

Yet, the kind of changes which James experienced as part of the life cycle, coupled with the intergenerational individual crises of his family, are not the only aspects of life which call for adaptability. Think of how much our culture has changed in this century and how much people have had to change as well. We live in a different world now than the one in which we started.

In the mid-1970's, I took my father, who was suffering from Alzheimer's, with me from Philadelphia to California where I was conducting a seminar. He had not flown since 1920 when he had taken his only flight in a bi-wing trainer. On our return trip, we made a stop in Atlanta. My father asked if we were home. I told him "not yet," but that we were in Atlanta and would arrive back in Philadelphia in less than two hours. He pondered my response and then said, in all seriousness, "Kid, this is the fastest train I've ever been on!"

My father's world had changed drastically. He had selectively chosen to ignore many of these changes, which affected how he experienced reality. Perhaps a less dramatic and more subtle illustration of the rapidity of change concerns my experience with computers. In 1986, when I moved to St. Louis, my subscription to *Personal Computing* ran out. I decided not to renew it until we had moved to our new home. I began reading the magazine again during the Spring of 1988. In less than two years, the personal computing industry had made such radical changes that I had to extensively expand my vocabulary and knowledge base in order to appreciate the articles more fully.

It occurred to me that a wonderful similarity exists between computers and humans. In the same way that computers can be upgraded to remain relevant and current, humans can also stay updated if they develop a biblical attitude toward change. For those who remain rigid towards change, they might be considered to be more like my old Tandy computer, which had extremely limited adaptability.

Is there a technique, an association, or a government program to enable us to process the changes of life gracefully? Or, are we the victims of chance upon whom life plays a series of bad jokes? Someone once observed that, "A lifetime of rich living should yield the ability to absorb change as it comes." The correctness of this comment is conditioned by the meaning of "rich living." If "rich living" means the development of a biblical world and life view integrated into one's practice of life, then it is true.

The best way to prepare for the changes which accompany aging is to learn how to think, act, and react biblically in daily life. The person who learns to live by the principles of Philippians 4:4-9 will not become captured by worry even when difficult events occur, such as being released involuntarily from his job at age 61. The principles of Philippians 4:4-9 are:

1. Rejoice in the Lord, rather than complain or rehearse the problem (v. 4).

2. To submit (root word here in Greek is gentleness) to God who is near (v. 5).

3. Stop worrying and start praying (v. 6).

4. Think right, or dwell upon the positive (v. 7).

5. Do right by obeying God and serving others (v. 9).

In addition to the major principles of Christian living, four specific guidelines can also aid us in aging gracefully.

Getting Right Makes You Right

If you are reading this, most likely you have had some type of a conversion experience. Through His Holy Spirit, God has convicted you of sin, regenerated your heart, and you have lifted up your empty hands of faith to say, "I believe in Jesus and His finished work on the cross for me." You have experienced reconciliation with God.

However, many Christians have not yet reconciled with their parents, siblings, or other significant people in their lives. One of the most important principles for aging gracefully includes "getting right makes you right." Someone living with unreconciled relationships does not have the good mental attitude it takes to age gracefully. Thank God, we can finally resolve these relationship problems--often after many years or decades.

Until later life, these problems often become masked by work, child-rearing, and other activities associated with the more demanding years of life. However, the increased leisure time, the decline in energy, and one's own impending death often bring these problems of youth and childhood closer to the surface. Bitterness and resentment frequently occur. An elderly individual, in looking back over his life, may remember such things as being molested as a child, treated unfairly, or abandoned. These types of memories are so vivid that they cannot be erased from the memory. However, you can face them and work through them biblically, even if the offending individual has died.

Getting these relationships right brings a person into a right relationship with the offending or offended party, the Lord God, and yourself. Reconciliation with significant others relieves our conscience and frees our energy for more positive living.

Contentment is Great Gain

We can grow old gracefully by learning the area of contentment. The Apostle Paul said from a jail cell, "I have learned to be content in whatever circumstances I am" (Philippians 4:11). Somewhere, one of the ancient Greek philosophers wrote, "He who is of a calm and happy nature will hardly feel the pressure of age."

To learn godly contentment means to learn to be at peace with the ebb and flow of life. Godly contentment, as seen in Paul's life, does not refer to inactivity or resignation to inevitable demise. Paul's life was an active life of ministry, despite the circumstances, while also trusting God to bring about His purposes.

Distinguish Between The Inevitable and The Opportunity

The Serenity Prayer

God grant me the SERENITY
to accept the things I cannot change;
COURAGE to change the things I can;
and WISDOM to know the difference--
Living one day at a time;
Enjoying one moment at a time;
Accepting hardships as the pathway to peace;
Taking, as He did, this sinful world
as it is, not as I would have it:
Trusting that He will make all things right
if I surrender to His Will;
That I may be reasonably happy in this life
and supremely happy with Him forever in the next. Amen.

Some change is thrust upon us. For example, one member of a couple will inevitably face the death of his or her mate. Retiring from a company is also inevitable for many individuals. Growing old gracefully depends upon distinguishing between these inevitable changes and the opportunities they present. By beginning to prepare for these changes, we can turn them into opportunities. Some people fight bereavement with anger, protest, or denial. In the process, they may become unreasonable, depressed and often present intolerable situations for the family. Others prepare themselves to accept the inevitable loss and refocus their lives. Then, having processed their loss, they move on to a new phase of life.

Learning biblical doctrine and talking with one's spouse about death and dying helps to prepare for the inevitable. Also, discussing retirement and making plans together helps with the changes that must take place.

In addition, growing older should include deciding to control the effects of aging by fighting against the decline in health, age discrimination, and other phenomena. These situations present us with challenges and opportunities that allow us to become gracefully adaptable in the process of aging.

A dear friend, we'll call him Joe, was released from his company when it was sold. He was 59 years old. He decided he could control the effects of his aging in this situation. He assembled a resume which highlighted his accomplishments and reflected the nature of his experience, while selectively deleting his age. He mounted a job campaign, which included the mailing of 200 professionally printed resumes. On the Monday following the Friday of his last week with his former company, Joe started his new job, having edged out several competing younger men.

Joe understood Romans 12:1-3. He took responsibility for his life and gracefully took positive action. With his life dedicated to the Lord and a proper view of himself, he prayerfully moved forward.

Part of growing older gracefully involves accepting that our Lord is still in the process of maturing us. One of the ways He causes us to grow is by allowing difficulties to come into our lives. With age comes an increase in difficulties for each of us. If we determine to adapt to these painful situations as Job did his, then we shall have a growth profile. Consider these statements from Job:

> "Though he slay me, yet will I trust him; but I will defend mine own ways before him" (13:15).
>
> "But he knoweth the way I take; when he hath tested men, I shall come forth as gold" (23:10).

Plan to Change

Do not plan to be disappointed. Having unrealistic expectations, such as simply relaxing and enjoying the fruits of your labors in peace and tranquillity, will only lead to boredom or disappointment. The game of life takes energy all the way to the end. Therefore, your plans need to be concrete and realistic. To put it another way, you must formulate attainable goals.

Joshua briefed the people of Israel as they readied to embark into the Promised Land saying, "You have not passed this way before. . . Consecrate yourselves. . . that you may know the way by which you shall go" (Joshua 3:4-5). We have not yet traveled the whole journey of life, but we are about to do so. Joshua's words of exhortation also apply to us. Consecration in the Old Testament scheme resulted in active preparation, not a passive utterance of the mouth. We need to consecrate ourselves for the aging phase of life in this Old Testament sense of the word.

Some years ago, we began to see young couples entering into marriage with little or no preparation. In recent years, the church has mounted Herculean efforts directed toward preparing young couples for marriage. However, the church has done very little to help prepare adults for the aging years. This study attempts to contribute to this planning.

From high school through the working cycle, one's time perception is molded by a vortex of activities. Each month and each year seems to come and go more rapidly. As a counselee once told me, "I plan 125 percent of my time. As a result, I never finish and can never relax." Such filling, or even overfilling, of one's schedule generates the perception that time flies. When you were 20, you wanted time to fly. The sooner graduation and your wedding arrived, the better. But at 50+, the relentless velocity of birthdays down the narrowing gorge of time becomes frightening.

At age 20 or 30, Scripture verses like "Redeem the time for the days are evil," or "Whatsoever your hand finds to do, do it heartily as unto the Lord," had time implications. What we understood from these verses was for us to do all that we can do as fast as we can do it. However, at age 50, what we might hear is to choose carefully, thoughtfully, and prayerfully what you spend your time doing, and savor each activity, recognizing that you are doing it for the Lord.

In other words, plan to fill your time with less activities, and enter into these activities with greater intensity and greater sensitivity. Allow yourself the time to treasure the many dimensions of God's handiwork in your life and through your life.

While planting a garden, I bemoaned the wait until harvest. A dear, gracious, Southern lady reminded me that the vegetables would be more tasty if I enjoyed the gardening process. She was right!

Planning is not something with which most people are unfamiliar. In fact, for many people, their schedules control them. They become captive to their plans.

Planning helps in the process of aging gracefully Planning helps to broaden a person's interest base. Not the kind of interest that accumulates on investments, although that is very important, but the interests which one develops in life. Often, after a person retires, he or she becomes bored, drives the family into a state of despair, and vegetates before the television. Research indicates that many people do, after retirement, the same things they did before they retired. Leisure without interests is not luxury. Without preparation for the enforced leisure of retirement, most people will not grow old gracefully. Although a pity, the common conception is that learning is for youth, work is for middle age, and leisure is for old age. The Christian conception of life represents a healthy balance of these three components throughout life.

5

CALEB'S CORPS

The name Ira D. Sankey is not a name commonly known. A biographical sketch of the well-known evangelist, Dwight L. Moody, would no doubt mention Sankey, but not in great detail. Yet, Sankey was an integral part of Moody's ministry, in much the same way Caleb was important in Joshua's ministry. Although Joshua's career in God's service encompasses a whole book by his name the commentary on Caleb's life is limited.

Caleb was the other "good guy" who gave a faithful and favorable report in response to his mission (Numbers 13:6, 20; 14:6) when the spies returned from the Promised Land. While Caleb's name is mentioned 32 times in six different Old Testament books, we still must assume the nature and amount of his contribution to Joshua's assignment as the successor of Moses. Like Sankey to Moody, the assumption of faithful and intense service of Caleb to Joshua certainly becomes warranted.

Several important items recorded in the Scriptures about Caleb and his actions should interest maturing adults in particular. Caleb is one of those biblical and historical characters whose life provides us with a model for Christian living. Rahab models the hope of redeeming faith for the dregs of society. Jacob models the possibility of character change, as shown by his name change from Jacob (the supplanter) to Israel. Peter offers a model of change to the common, coarse, and arrogant man. However, Caleb offers us a unique model. He represents a model of vigor, vigilance, and victory for the maturing adult. Caleb's Corps consists of a congregation of conquering senior adults.

Looking at the life of Caleb, we discover that he was 40 years old when his first exploit of godly service was recorded. Caleb approached Joshua (Joshua 14:6-9) to remind him of Moses' promise of an inheritance in the Promised Land. While speaking with Joshua, we are told that he was 40 years old when he was first commissioned as one of the spies. Undoubtedly, Caleb became involved in Israel's religious life just prior to this assignment to the spy brigade. He was, at the very least, a ruler in Israel (Numbers 13:2-3). In Israel's theocracy, the position of ruler was religious in nature. However, we have no indication that Caleb was a man of any greater spiritual development or personal character than any of the others chosen by Moses for this mission.

The commission was given (Numbers 13:17), the mission was planned (Numbers 13:18-20), and the plan was executed (Numbers 13:21-25). Caleb, along with Joshua, was challenged by the opportunity. His faith was stretched to pursue God's Promised Land. Whatever the level of his spiritual condition previously, we observe that, from mid-life forward, faith and consecration characterize his life.

Faith
(Numbers 13:30)

Faith refers to the necessary ingredient of success for the Christian. Faith represents that quality of character by which we believe God's promises and act upon them. Faith also sees obstacles as God's opportunities to demonstrate His power. Faith sees problems as challenges and complications as curves in the road. Faith sees delays as a sovereign God's timing, and faith understands frustrations to be the tools of a sanctifying Father.

Caleb had faith. The description of the majority report (Numbers 13:28-29) of the obstacles to taking the Promised Land would elicit the two responses recorded. The majority response was fear, yet Caleb responded with faith.

Can you not hear the majority?

"Yes, this is a great land. But the people are well fortified. One race that lives among them are all giants. If we go up against them, it is sheer disaster. Our belongings will be confiscated. Our women will be misused. Our children will become slaves and we will be killed. If God wants us to have that land, He'll have to clean out those pagans first."

Caleb can hold his peace no longer. He jumps to his feet and cries out, "Let us go at once and occupy it; for we are well able to overcome it" (Numbers 13:20).

The majority answer him with a chorus of protest stirring the emotions of the nation. Mass hysteria sets in (Numbers 14:1-3). Moses and Aaron humble themselves before the people (Numbers 14:5). The faith of Caleb and Joshua motivates them to risk their lives and challenge the entire nation (Numbers 14:6-10). Their faith in the power of God appears to be clearly evident here.

Faith in God is the key element for those who would join Caleb's Corps. Finances, health, objections of family and friends, ridicule for lack of specific training, and other obstacles will stand in your way, but only faith in the God of the universe will provide you with the capacity to overcome. Sometimes, God may even delay or circumscribe your accomplishments by the lack of faith in those around you, just as he did in Caleb's case.

In difficult circumstances, remember Caleb's example. He was faithful through 40 years while God disciplined the rest of the nation. His faith did not wane. He was ready to take his mountain when they got to the Promised Land.

Consecration

(Joshua 14:8-9; Deuteronomy 1:36)

Since of all the annotations which refer to Caleb's obedience to God date after his experience on the spying expedition, we have good reason to understand this encounter to be a life changing episode. He had to face the choice of either going with the majority (Numbers 13:28-29), whose interpretation of reality left God out, or becoming the articulate minority willing to view the challenges of life through faith in God (Numbers 13:30; 14:5-9).

The majority were not ready to move on God's promise. They already had not believed God nine times (Numbers 14:22) and desired to go back to Egypt rather than trust God to go before them and defeat the enemy. No doubt Caleb realized that he was laying his life on the line when he made his minority report and later pled with the people not to side with the majority report (Numbers 14:10).

Consecration occurs at those times when a Christian presents his life as a "living sacrifice" to God (Romans 12:1-2). While this is a significant event in the life of a believer, it is important to specify what that consecration means from time to time as well. This incident in Caleb's life caused him to define what it meant for him to be consecrated. He made a conscious decision and a public declaration of his intent to follow the Lord, regardless of the cost.

We must also understand that Caleb's response of faith and consecration did not result in immediate personal blessing. He was assured that he would not die in the wilderness with the rebels. However, he had to wander around the wilderness, live on manna, and put up with the regular occasions of disobedience on the part of Israel and the punishments which resulted. If you are in Caleb's Corps, or if you decide to join it, remember that you should not expect things to go well all of a sudden. Often, those whom you serve will forget to thank you, or they may even curse you.

In Caleb, we find encouragement for all of us, during mid-life and beyond. In various ways and at various times, the Lord brings experiences that allow us to make course corrections in our lives--opportunities to express faith and consecrate ourselves to follow Him fully.

Caleb's Corps is populated by those who, in mid-life, make such a course correction. This study could present someone with an opportunity to make such a life changing decision. The quiet response of the heart to the "still small voice" brings glory of God. Traumatic experiences, or special occasions such as a trip to the mission field, are all opportunities to hear that still, small voice.

Those who join Caleb's Corps may do so by following another example set by him. In Joshua 14:10, we note Caleb's determination to assume a most strenuous task while trusting the Lord to enable him to complete it. Caleb was 85 when he came to Joshua and said, "Give me this mountain."

We will encounter an assortment of mountains to be taken for the Lord during our lifetimes. Many senior adults have the unique opportunities to take these mountains for the Lord and His church.

These opportunities arise out of the uniqueness of our Western culture. God has abundantly blessed us materially. Retirement programs, coupled with Social Security programs and personal investments, have the potential to free hundreds of thousands of older Americans to conquer such "mountains." The question for nearly every older adult at some point in his life is not "Shall I conquer a mountain?" but, "Which mountain shall I conquer?"

To help you think through the challenge of joining Caleb's Corps, the following is a project to enable you to identify some possible mountains, as well as some questions you need to answer:

1. List ten mountains that senior adults can conquer.

2. Questions that are important to any conqueror:

   a. What kind of attitudes does a conqueror possess?
   b. What kind of sacrifices does a conqueror make?
   c. What kind of resources does a conqueror need access to?

3. Develop an application for each of these questions for senior adults. Be specific.

   a. How can senior adults develop the attitudes of a conqueror?
   b. What actual sacrifices might senior adults have to make in order to conquer their mountains?
   c. What resources do senior adults have to enable them to conquer these mountains?

6

WEARINESS IN WELL DOING:
A Study in Overcoming

Charles has served as an active church member since he came to know the Lord during a period of serious marital conflict 30 years ago. Their pastor counseled with Charles and Sue for several months, during which time they both learned to understand a more godly approach to marriage and communication. They have set good examples for others to follow and have counseled other young couples for many years.

Recently, Charles approached his pastor to indicate that he no longer desired to teach a married couples Sunday School Class or to continue other leadership responsibilities. He shared with the pastor that the difficulty with his hearing had grown worse and interfered with his performance.

As they talked, it became evident that Charles had been frustrated for some time. He had concluded that the only solution was to withdraw from the ministry.

John was asked to serve as the coordinator of the new building fund drive. John had always wanted to serve as a project man for the session or pastor. His work had required him to travel extensively. John often said, "Projects are something I can do by myself, and traveling gives me a wide exposure to fresh ideas from other parts of the country." His wife, Mary, commented that John's experience at church had always been very positive.

John qualified for the new assignment, both by his job experience and his spiritual track record. Having retired two months earlier, John gladly accepted the challenge and looked forward to working closely with the others on the committee. Now, after three months of struggling with two deacons "who are always negative, shortsighted, and have no faith at all in money matters," John said, "I am resigning, Pastor. I'm too old to put up with this kind of hassle. I've fought these kinds of people-problems for 45 years in business. I don't need it in the church."

In this chapter, we will look at several older men in Hebrew history. Each faced a particular kind of problem which God allowed. These stories indicate common problems which are frequently seen in the lives of older adults. Let's see how the Lord wants us to face such challenges.

Physical Problems

Moses experienced each of the type of problems under consideration today. However, in this chapter, we will only focus on his physical condition.

Moses was about 80 years old when the angel of the Lord appeared to him in the burning bush (Exodus 3:5). The Lord began this encounter with a warning that Moses stood on holy ground. He continued by identifying Himself (Exodus 3:6) and appraising Moses of His intent to free Israel (Exodus 3:7). Following this awesome opener, God simply tells Moses, "So now, go, I am sending you to Pharaoh to bring my people...out of Egypt" (Exodus 3:10).

Even though it seems incredible, Moses responded with a series of questions and reasons why God should not send him to free Israel. In Exodus 3:1, he asks the question: "Who am I?" Moses missed the implication of the commission in light of who was giving it. If the President of the United States should give an order to a private in the Army of the United States, that private must then carry out that commission, not by virtue of his own personage or rank, but by the personage and rank of him who gave the commission. If God calls Christians to do a job, who those Christians are is not important. Their gifts and abilities, their educational backgrounds, and their experiences may help, but they are not the determining factors. God's people should never forget that a shoe salesman, D. L. Moody, with no formal education for ministry, soon became the greatest evangelist of the 19th century.

Moses' second question, "What is your name?" (Exodus 3:13), was an unnecessary question since the Lord had already identified Himself in verse six. If Moses needed a name beyond "I am the God of your fathers," the Lord would have already given it to him. When God answered Moses by stating that he was to tell the Israelites that "I am has sent you," He only puts in verbal form what He had already implied.

Moses' third question may reflect a lack of faith. If God had sent him and assured him of success (Exodus 3:15-22), then surely Israel's believing him became God's problem, not Moses'. However, the flow of the text seems to indicate that Moses sought to be equipped for a likely contingency. The Lord responded by demonstrating the supernatural enhancements with which He endowed Moses (Exodus 4:1-9).

Moses' next question angers the Lord. What is different about this question? Perhaps its formulation as a statement sparks God's anger. Moses' statement seems to say, "Here is something you don't have an answer to or a problem you have not thought of." Such thinking or assumption shows lack of faith and confidence in God (Exodus 4:10). After answering each of Moses' previous questions patiently, while instructing and assuring him, God shows displeasure with this question. Most major commentators agree that Moses suffered from a speech impediment -- a physical weakness. The Lord pointed out to Moses that He is the Creator and is completely in charge of this problem. However, just to reassure Moses, God also promised an assistant speaker to help him (Exodus 4:11-17).

As we age, we develop physical problems which can impair our service. The Lord is our Creator, in control of our physical problems, and may provide healing, directly or indirectly through medicine. At other times, if God chooses not to heal our physical problems, we need to look for our "Aaron" whom God may supply to help us as we serve. We must neither lose faith in the God who has commissioned us, nor make the assumption that He cannot enable us to carry out His commission.

Performance Problems

In the business world, employees commonly experience a yearly performance review. In the New Testament, Christians are called upon to do frequent spiritual performance reviews. For example, Paul challenges participants of the Lord's Table to do a spiritual performance review before partaking of the elements of this sacrament. Performance problems are common to all Christians, but in Genesis 17 and 18, Moses records a particular performance problem that may be common to Christians of advancing years.

Abraham, the Scripture says, "Believed God and it was accounted to him for righteousness" (Genesis 15:6; Galatians 3:6). He is held up to be the model of performance with respect to faith. Yet, he had a problem with Christian performance in the area of faith. Could God do the impossible as He was promising? Abraham had believed that God would somehow give him an heir from his own body. However, years later, at age 100, when God again said that He would give him a son with his 90-year-old wife Sarah, Abraham had a performance problem. He "fell upon his face and laughed" (Genesis 17:17).

Sarah followed Abraham's example when three angels appeared at their tent and reaffirmed God's promise of a son. In Genesis 18:12, we see that Sarah laughed to herself at the suggestion that she should enjoy her husband at her advanced age and become pregnant.

Performance problems with respect to specific faith demands are very common as Christians age. They do not have difficulty believing God for salvation, or even for the supply of worldly needs, but, in specific areas in which they perceive the aging process to be a problem, "laughter" replaces faith.

James had good "performance reviews" since his conversion at age 20. Within three months, he had absorbed the catechism instruction by his faithful pastor and had accepted the challenge to be an assistant teacher in the Youth Department. After graduation from college, he took his engineering degree to Detroit and rode the postwar auto wave to the top ranks, retiring as a chief engineer. During all these years of success, James continued to perform in his personal Christian life and in his Christian service. He was known as a ruling elder who spent much time ministering to people. He had little taste for long session meetings, which he referred to as "much ado about nothing."

Three months after retirement, James was approached by his pastor and a much younger session member who had long admired James and unconsciously modeled his approach to being an elder after James' example. Over breakfast, they confided in James their desire to propose the planting of a daughter church to the session.

"The men will not buy our idea at this time if it includes hiring another minister. We have, as you know, been blessed with sufficient growth this year to reach the 80 percent saturation point of our facilities, and they are only a year and a half old. We thank God for the great opportunity He has given to us. But along with the people blessing, He has not yet given us the financial blessing to liquidate our debt. To acquire more property and build again is not possible," concluded Pastor Jones.

"That's right," continued Frank, "but I have contacted the Seventh Day Adventist Church close by my house. They have not only agreed to rent their facility to us on Sunday, but have also offered us Tuesday or Thursday evening. All of this will cost only $100.00 a month, plus a utility charge to be determined by the increase of their bill by our use. With Pastor Jones' permission, I have confidentially talked with ten of our young couples who live out our way, and three older couples who are willing to give three years to us so that we will have some maturity in our group. They were all excited about the possibility of planting another congregation as a part of our church's extension."

"James, Frank and I have prayed for several weeks about this matter. On Monday, I mentioned to him that your name kept coming to my mind each time I prayed. He said he was not surprised because he was having the same experience. I know, James, that you can hold your own in most theological discussions with any seminary graduate. You have spent, what, five, five-week stints studying with R. C. Sproul? You've been to Pensacola Institute on a number of occasions. I've seen you reading church growth books, and you've been most helpful to me in teaching these principles to our people. You've preached regularly in my absence. I almost felt threatened when I had to take those six weeks off for surgery because you preached that series on forgiveness so well."

"James, we would like to take a plan to the session to initiate another congregation. We'd like to list the thirteen families committed to the project, and we'd like to present you to the session as the elder, lay minister, to carry out the ministry. We would also like to recommend the title, Minister of Church Planting, with a full staff role. We would have in view recommending you for ordination by special exception after one year. The only catch is that we have no money in the budget from which we can recommend a salary at this time; however, we do have sufficient money in the general budget to recommend leasing a car for you and covering your other auto expenses. We trust that the Lord has provided sufficiently for your present needs through your pension and Social Security."

James expressed his surprise, but he did agree to pray about it. As he drove home from the meeting, he laughed to himself and thought, "After a life time of engineering cars, these guys want me to become a people person and a salesman."

Pride Problems

The third problem which seems to be prevalent among Christians of advancing years concerns pride. Somehow, older Christians who have received great blessings materially, spiritually, and physically tend to forget the source of their good "fortune" and become presumptive of their blessings. Two kings of Judah are instructive to us at this point.

In 2 Chronicles 26, we find the ascension of Uzziah at the age of 16 to the throne of Israel. In verse four, the wonderful commentary on this man's life is, ". . . he did right in the sight of the Lord." From verses 5 through 15, the writer records his many accomplishments, which resulted from the fact that "while he sought the Lord, God prospered him."

However, Uzziah lost sight of the fact that his success came from the Lord. We also see here that "when he became strong, his heart was so proud that he acted corruptly" (2 Chronicles 26:16). His corrupt action involved invading the priestly role and attempting to burn incense in the temple.

Some years later, Uzziah's great- great-grandson, Hezekiah, followed his example (2 Chronicles 32). Sennacherib, King of Assyria, had Judah, including Jerusalem, under siege. In verse 20, he recounts that Isaiah had joined Hezekiah in prayer. God's response was to dispatch an angel who destroyed the Assyrian army (2 Chronicles 32:21). As a result of this blessing, the other nations honored Hezekiah for defeating Assyria.

Unfortunately, his pride was a heart attitude (2 Chronicles 32: 25). Even Hezekiah's personal experience of God's healing and granting 15 additional years of life did not heal his attitude problem. According to the Scriptures, the Lord allowed the visit of the envoys from Babylon (2 Kings 20:12-21) to test him and reveal his heart attitude. Hezekiah repented of his pride at this point, but his attitude had already set in motion the circumstances that would result in the fall of Jerusalem after his death.

The book of Proverbs gives this warning: "Pride goes before a fall" (Proverbs 18:18). Aging adults may have it easy in this American society. We can drive our vacation homes from one national park to another, board a plane for Scotland or Hawaii, or purchase a new Honda Accord with our retirement bonus. But we tend to forget the source of our success by failing to give God the credit and praise. We may also find it easy to forget that the Lord has endowed us with good minds, provided us a society structured around moral qualities which have enhanced our opportunities for success, provided the personal network of people who have contributed to our promotions, and led us in decisions which have produced personal growth and development. In short, we may even develop prideful attitudes about who we are and what we have acquired.

Such pride requires repentance and should drive us to our knees to ask our Lord for mercy so that our children and grandchildren will not suffer from this same pride. The recognition of such pride should humble us and encourage us to devise ways to develop and to maintain humble attitudes, by always giving our God credit for the successes of life.

Paul teaches us that we should "occupy till He comes." This obviously refers to a military allusion of maintaining control over a given geographic area. The implication is that resistance will continue. As believers, we are in enemy territory. Remember that

Satan is the god of this world. Often we become weary with the struggle associated with occupying "captured territory." In this chapter, we have identified physical, performance and pride problems that may contribute to weariness as we grow older. As my mother often used to say, "a stitch in time saves nine." I pray that bringing these vulnerable areas to your awareness will serve as a stitch to prevent the tear of weariness in well-doing.

7

INTERGENERATIONAL INTERDEPENDENCE

A Bible study in the Old Testament of the phrases "little ones" and "the people" suggests very strongly that God viewed Israel as a corporate unity. Among the topics mentioned here include the following: intergenerational responsibility, education, blessing (Deuteronomy 27-28), and judgment (Numbers 16:26-32). The study of ancient Jewish culture leaves little doubt that 12-year-old males learned adult responsibility. The Deuteronomy 27 passage also clearly implies that children shared in the instruction of the nation.

We might appreciate this scene even more if we envision Moses and the elders teaching a giant Sunday school class. Hundreds of family units make up each class. Father, mother, and children for several generations gathered in a common class. The subject of the lesson focuses on God's commands and the blessings and curses for obedience and disobedience. It would do the text no harm to suppose that these families gathered around the table at the next meal and discussed the "lesson" in detail. Surely children had questions, those simple, penetrating questions uninhibited by adult "sophistication." Adults must have expressed their fear, concern, surprise, confusion, and speculation of God's blessings or curses to come. We should further suppose that those simple questions that the children asked precipitated soul-searching on behalf of the adults. The adult responses, in turn, would generate serious reflection on the part of the children. Here, then, is intergenerational Christian education at its best.

Most likely, the institution and celebration of the Passover provided a wonderful intergenerational experience for Israel. On the night before the Exodus, when Moses led approximately three million people out of Egypt, the Passover was instituted. Though we are to understand that all Jewish families participated in the Passover, we should not think that everyone fully understood its meaning. As they enacted that saving ritual, many questions floated around the table. I suppose that parents and grandparents felt stimulated to explore the Passover's fuller meaning because of the children's questions. When allowed to participate in adult conversations, children can often teach the adults.

Carol LeAnn, age 12, turned to her father on the way home from a Sunday communion service. "Daddy," she asked, "isn't communion like Jewish Passover?"

"Well, I guess. I'm not sure," replied her father.

John, Carol LeAnn's maternal grandfather, chimed into the conversation. "Yes, it is. The Passover looked forward to the coming of the Lamb of God, who is our Lord Jesus Christ. The Passover lamb's blood saved the first-born of each faithful Jewish family. Our communion service looks back to Jesus and His death on the cross for us, "

"Well, just what do you mean?" asked Carol LeAnn's father.

"I think, Daddy, that the Passover became a reminder to the nation of Israel that the blood of a perfect lamb was shed for their deliverance. The communion reminds us that Jesus' blood was shed for us."

"Say, that is pretty good theology, young lady," responded her grandfather. "You are giving your daddy some right smart instruction."

That similar scenes occurred around the Old Testament Passover table is certain. Many understood very little about the Passover process, especially after its practice had become passé. When the celebration was recovered, they had ample occasion for intergenerational learning as a result.

We can see another example of intergenerational interdependency in the account of Paul, Barnabas, and John Mark (Acts 15:36-41). Paul had taken John Mark on a missionary expedition. For an unstated reason, John Mark left Paul's company and returned home. On a later occasion, Barnabas wanted to take John Mark on another endeavor, but Paul refused. Their differences became so strong that Paul took Silas and departed in one direction, and Barnabas took John Mark and departed in another direction. Barnabas' name means "encourager." He lived out the meaning of his name in relation to young John Mark, who was probably a generation younger than Barnabas. The success of intergenerational interdependency became apparent in John Mark's Christian maturity. While John Mark depended upon Barnabas to argue his case and defend him, Barnabas depended upon John Mark to be teachable and become dependable. We see this in Paul's later admission that John Mark had become beneficial to him in his ministry.

Older adults who have more time and less demands upon them have a great opportunity presented to them. Many younger people can profit from a calm, firm hand, a steady, understanding voice, and a mature ability to make and teach good judgment. While it may take some time to win the young person's confidence, when you have won his or her willingness to listen, the influence which you can exercise becomes very great.

Joseph provides an instructive study of intergenerational interdependency. By God's grace, Joseph overcame the evil of his brothers. He became his brothers' teacher and his father's caretaker. In fact, Joseph's whole family was dependent upon his mercy (Genesis 47:1-11). Joseph taught them all respect for authority, the practice of mercy (Genesis 45:1-5), and the character of God (Genesis 45:6-8).

Stop reading for a few minutes and list some situations in which people can experience intergenerational interdependency. Some examples to stimulate your thinking are:

1. When older adults have a divorced child with small children, these grandparents may assist in the rearing of their grandchildren. This is the actual situation quite frequently, but the question is, "How intergenerational is this process that actually goes on?" Sometimes it is a baby-sitting service that is as impersonal as paid help. How can this be turned into an intergenerational, interdependent experience?

2. Grandchildren can help with the upkeep and care of their grandparents' home. Children of the church can aid older adults in the church with these same tasks.

3. A well-traveled, self-taught senior adult (my father-in-law, for example, has acquired a knowledge of the history of Scotland equivalent to that of a college professor) may augment the high school or middle-school teacher with the teaching of this segment in the class.

4. A senior adult couple who has lived through one of life's tragedies, such as the death of a child, raising a physically challenged child, or experiencing the loss of a fortune, may be useful in teaching a high school or college class. They can lead the class through the experience, how it affected them, how they learned to deal with it, what lessons God taught them, and the perspective that time has given them on the situation.

When the Presbyterian Church of America administers a baptism, the Book of Church Order prescribes that the minister present the congregation with a challenge to take a vow of assistance. Listen to what the congregation pledges to perform:

> "Do you, as a congregation, undertake the responsibility of assisting the parents in the Christian nurture of this child?"

Here we see a significant, intergenerational solemn vow. The entire congregation most likely includes people of all ages, from children through senior adults. Each makes a vow to assist the presenting parents in the awesome task of parenting.

In reality, the nomenclature of this chapter does not introduce a unique concept to the Christian life. Intergenerational interdependency simply refers to a way to refocus our attention on the biblical picture of the body of Christ. In 1 Corinthians 12 and Romans 12, the Apostle Paul has taught the Christian church that believers are interdependent, just as the members of the physical body are. Each member has a unique set of functions and abilities to benefit the body. No one in the body can play down his own role or function nor that of another individual. Paul's illustration places no age limits on the functions of individuals within the church. By its context and definition, the church is intergenerational in nature.

This chapter has simply cast this ageless truth of God's creative order in contemporary terminology. Let the Holy Spirit illumine your mind and challenge your heart afresh. Work at making the application practical. If left to our own human devices, we tend to become generationally ingrown. Age-graded and perpetual Sunday School classes lead to such ingrownness. Furthermore, an independent spirit (until life forces us to become dependent upon another generation) shields us from experiencing the interdependence which God intended to be a part of our Christian experience.

How can we make this intergenerational interdependence a more functional reality in today's church? How can senior adults interface with middle-aged adults, younger adults, teens, and children? Answering these questions would probably make a good group exercise. To prime your thinking, I have developed a few situations which have provided such "intergenerationalism."

One church developed a summer day camp program. Unlike most such operations, this church staffed from within itself. The director was a middle-aged lady, and her co-director was an older adult. The staff was incremental in utilizing college, senior high, and junior high students. All were paid staff. This raised the value of the positions and put everyone in the role of being a "real" staff person regardless of age. The staff also included several older folks who, while volunteers, functioned as paid staff. What a great team! A true interdependency existed, where growth and learning between all members of the staff occurred.

A similar scene took place in a VBS program some years ago. For reasons long forgotten, but no doubt very common, our church was short of adult volunteers. High school and junior high students, as well as several senior adults, were recruited. It was a great experience, with over 500 children enrolled. The highlight of the week was an older man who was the roving storyteller. Several teenage boys expressed the extent of the impact this gentleman had upon them during the week. The storyteller shared how he had been spiritually and personally refreshed through his ministry to the children.

A church where I was serving produced a stage adaption of "The Light and The Glory." One of the great joys of this experience was working with high school students through senior adults. I found it exciting to watch the chemistry between these various ages.

The Christian education flyer from one church included the following intergenerational Sunday school class:

> "Pairs and Spares: Teens to retired, with and without children and grandchildren! A diverse group of people, actively participating in class, learning from each other. Bible study and daily living is emphasized. This class participates in service projects. Occasional social activities are planned."

So how can the church generate the enrichment that comes from intergenerational interdependence? First, it must be committed to a philosophy that is intergenerational.. Second, people of all ages must be recruited to participate in small fellowship groups. Finally, a church can begin to understand the importance of intergenerational interdependence through individuals like you promoting such a concept in his or her own life.

8

CAREGIVING AND THE CHRISTIAN COMMUNITY

It is a biblical reality that all mankind will age. The mind, the body, and the emotional structure deteriorates (review the aging process of King David, the man "after God's own heart," 1 Kings 1:1 - 2:1). We begin life needing the caregiving of a loving, tender mother and a strong, loving father to provide for the development of our minds, the feeding and grooming of our bodies, and the caressing of our emotional selves. At 70 or 80 we need love no less than we did in early childhood. As we reach toward the extremity of life, caregiving dependency on others progressively returns. We may need the assistance of someone younger to compensate for our deteriorating minds and our ill-functioning bodies. We shall also continue to need emotional affirmation, just as we did as children.

The closing years of Jacob's and Joseph's lives provide some gerontological insights. In particular, they reflect caregiving at an intergenerational level. In Genesis 45:9-11, we read Joseph's instructions to his brothers after their emotional reunion in Egypt.

> "Hurry and go up to my father, and say to him, 'Thus says your son Joseph: God has made me lord of all Egypt; come down to me; do not tarry. You shall dwell in the land of Goshen, and you shall be near me, you and your children, your children's children, your flocks and your herds, and all that you have. There I will provide for you. . . .'"

Though Jacob proclaimed his readiness for death after his reunion with Joseph, the Lord gave him 17 more years of life. He lived these years of frailty with his extended family, which provided care for him. As evidenced in Genesis 47:27-31, he continued to play a vital part in family structure, even at the point of being sick unto death. Chapters 48 and 49 record very important family interactions. Jacob, exercising his cultural role as patriarch, provided structure to his family to ensure peaceful relationships after his death.

In Genesis 50:17-21, Joseph's brothers approached him after their father's death, out of guilt and fear. Now that their father had died, Joseph's retribution for his brother's earlier mistreatment of him became a distinct possibility, but Joseph assured them that the past was in God's providence. He then promised his brothers that "I will provide for you and your little ones." If you remember, Joseph was one of the youngest sons of Jacob. While exact chronology is difficult, Joseph was probably in his 90's when his father died. Joseph promised his elderly brothers the necessary caregiving they needed. Until his death at 110, Joseph's family was very much involved in his life and he in theirs, as we see in Genesis 50:23.

While the major intent of this biblical material is not to instruct us regarding the caregiving process of older adults, it certainly reflects how these godly families, with all their foibles, cared for their aging members. When we remember that this large, extended family also belonged to the community of God, the examples become instructive to the church as well as the community.

We can definitely see the need for this type of instruction. The numbers of us who will live sufficiently long enough to return to the care-receiving stage continue to increase rapidly. The prospective impact of these numbers stuns those Americans who study trends. Even the popular press has sounded a warning note. "Right now, 1 in 8 Americans is 65 or over. By 2030, almost 1 in 5 will be over 65. People 85 and over represent one of the fastest growing age groups" (Wall Street Journal, 12/9/86).

Our culture has responded by creating institutions to provide for the basic needs of the infirm. Until recently, we have delegated the caregiving responsibility far too frequently to in-house professional services. These institutions are intended to solve the problem of bodily needs, but they frequently provide sparingly for the elderly's mental and emotional needs. We find it heartwrenching to see people with minimal needs institutionalized. These people lose their freedom of choice, their familiar surroundings, and the emotional support of their families, friends, and churches. They are often left with a void.

We find it alarming to note that a large number of Americans are unnecessarily or prematurely consigned to nursing homes. One senior adult care specialist observed that his years of experience caused him to question 50 percent of the nursing home placements at the time they were made. Many of these placements could have been postponed for at least six months. While a guess may not be wise, it certainly seems likely that a good percentage of that 50 percent who were prematurely placed in a nursing home might never have seen the inside of the nursing home had the placement been postponed.

If personal care assistance would have been available, many of these families could have provided the care needed. Unfortunately, the community or the church does not often provide such an alternative. When the only alternative for the family is nursing home placement, the senior adult, the family, and the church all suffer the consequences.

The family prematurely loses the benefits of the normal family interaction. Children can no longer play games with the grandparent. Family meals and events also have an empty place. The senior adult member must make a transition to another phase of life before the actual demands of his or her condition dictate it. This phase includes the loss of regular family support. Having the night nurse who is just doing her job adjust the pillow is quite different than having a loving daughter adjust the same pillow.

The church also suffers loss. Mary Sue's bright face is missing from her regular pew. The children miss her attention as well. Her godly prayers, which encouraged everyone in prayer meeting, are sorely missed. When the transition to the nursing home becomes necessary, the nursing home seems like a blessing to all. However, when it is premature, it yields a loss to all.

The benefits of life always result from the investment of ourselves. Even God's blessings flow through our or another's obedience. This principle does not change when it comes to caring for senior adults. The adult children provide much of the care for senior adults at the same time they often must care for their own children or have returned to work to produce income for the children's college expenses. The needs of elderly parents can grow enormous, generating unbelievable burdens for the caregivers. Most of these caregivers are women. They exhaust time and energy needed by their husbands and children in caring for their aged parents. When these contingencies are short-term, the family grows by the "stretching experience." The family learns patience and cooperation (James 1:2-5). However, when the short-term becomes the norm, the family reserves are constantly under pressure. While the Christian family can endure through the enabling hand of God, the quality of life enjoyed is diminished as a result.

The church, which takes its responsibility seriously, also suffers exhausting demands. The overload on staff and volunteer labor leads to individual burnout as the church tries to minister to an ever increasing constituency of frail elderly. Metropolitan churches cover a large geographical area. When these churches are located in the city, they frequently have a large population of elderly who live close to the church. However, the younger individuals who are the volunteer staff often live in the suburbs. The driving distances and the commuting time to provide a basic ministry to these older adults becomes prohibitive. In the process, the church suffers the loss of its ability to minister to these individuals.

Jesus Christ cares about His hurting people. He said, "Inasmuch as you have done it unto one of the least of these my brethren you have done it unto me" (Matthew 25:40). If you have ever visited some nursing homes or have seen some of the elderly street people in major cities, you have seen just how `least' some of these individuals are. We need to be imitators of our Lord Jesus Christ in caring for the needy.

What are the alternatives available to us who care? One of the choices for us is through personal care assistance. I will discuss this subject at length in another chapter. Here we simply mention it so that we can see it as a way of postponing the nursing home necessity.

Another alternative is not to leave all of the caregiving of the nursing home residents to the professional staff. Families need to see the nursing home as a place that does for them what they cannot do, not a place that does all they do not want to do. Placing our frail, or not so frail, relative in the nursing home does not absolve us of the responsibility for their mental and emotional needs. When the family must move toward the nursing home in order to meet the care needs of a relative, it should see the nursing home as an augmentation of itself. We should also see the staff as part of the family team, playing the positions the family cannot play.

Still another alternative exists. Just as the family is not free of responsibility for the well-being of the nursing home resident, the church also is not. The church, that is, the individuals who are members of the church, should have an organized methodology for providing ministry to their members in nursing homes. However, we are not only to minister to our own, but to the community as well. Therefore, every church should seek to have a ministry to nursing home residents.

In many instances, the people most able to provide such a ministry include those who themselves are Prime-Timers (senior adults). This is also an excellent ministry to cross-pollinate older adults and teenagers. Together, they can provide a unique ministry which enriches the nursing home resident, the older adult, and the teenager. You may have heard that the heart grows colder to spiritual matters as people grow older. Don't you believe it. This is especially not true in the nursing home where, in a short time, many have had to reduce life accomplishments to three drawers and a three-foot closet. The fleeting value of the temporal sets in rather quickly, and eternal truths are renewed. Many indeed are "white unto harvest."

Caregiving becomes a necessity for a dying humanity, especially as a Christian virtue. Caregiving depends on all of the Christian graces and many times receives little in return. Even the satisfaction of serving can sometimes be overshadowed by the enormous drain. Often, the satisfaction is realized after the task is completed. Caregiving to the older adult will continue to place an increasing demand on the Christian community for generations to come. Only an aggressive posture will help the church and the individual meet this challenge.

9

ENDOWED WITH DIGNITY

In my 9th grade biology class my teacher displayed good teaching technique when he gave an excited affirmation to a classmate who had observed, "You mean man is an animal, and that is why he is at the top of the taxonomic chart?" To his affirmation, the student replied, "Well, maybe you are an animal, but I'm not."

Christianity sees man and animals as qualitatively different. While, biologically, many similarities of design exist, we are still uniquely created in the image of God. This *Imago Dei* gives man dignity. Observe this basis of dignity from the Word of God. The words dignity, honor, and respect are used synonymously in this chapter.

God Endows with Dignity

The book of beginnings records God's decision to create man (Genesis 1:26-31). The endowment with dignity actually has three aspects associated with it. First and foremost, we were created in God's image. This creation in God's image sets people apart from all other creatures. With God-like qualities, we were endowed with dignity in His very existence.

As a consequence of our creation in the image of God, God gave us two assignments which set us apart from the rest of creation and contribute to our endowment with dignity. God gave us all the ability and responsibility to enter into God's creative work. "Be fruitful and multiply" implies both ability and responsibility to create new image-bearers through the reproductive process.

We find the third aspect of dignity in our assigned cultural mandate. We have the responsibility to "subdue" and "have dominion" over the earth and all living creatures.

Notice that each of these responsibilities depends upon the unique abilities of people, which depends upon our unique creation in God's image. In other words, while we do have dignity, it is a *derived* dignity. Every human being possesses this honor with which God has endowed us. At the same time, we become humble before God and exalted by God. God has endowed us with dignity and treats us with dignity.

God Protects Dignity

In Genesis 9:6, God established the law of capital punishment. Our task here is not to debate the pros and cons of capital punishment. We only want to observe God's intent to preserve respect of one man in his total being for another man in his total being.

From a simple reading of this passage, it seems clear that God's intent is to protect the image of God. What makes murder inexcusable is that the image bearer of God is destroyed. The very heart of one's dignity is cut out. One can no longer represent God or carry out his Godlike functions of creation and dominion. Hence, God established the law of capital punishment to protect one's dignity by giving society the responsibility to punish murder and thereby deter it.

God Directs Dignity

Many examples exist of God teaching us how to preserve the dignity of other human beings. For example, the Old Testament law of gleaning gave the poor an opportunity to provide for themselves through the work of collecting grain from the fields of the more fortunate (Leviticus 19:10; Ruth 2:7). Also, in the New Testament, we find it particularly instructive to observe His direction with reference to how we speak to one another.

Two New Testament passages speak with clarity about the tongue. In Ephesians 4:29-32, the Apostle Paul has addressed a number of problems which are expressed through speaking.. Verse 31 gives a list of items to be "put off" or removed from one's behavior. Each of these refers to interpersonal interactions. Listen to Paul:

> "Let all bitterness, and wrath, and anger, and clamor, and evil speaking, be put away from you, with all malice . . ."

However, one word here does not fit this pattern in the original language. In the Greek New Testament, this is not a neat package referring to interpersonal relationships. The "evil speaking" is actually the word "blaspheme." To blaspheme means to speak evil against God, that is, to speak against the dignity of God. What is Paul's point, then? It is this. When bitterness, anger, wrath, and clamor give way to attacking another human being, the attack is actually against God. When one human being attacks the dignity of another human being, he or she, in fact, attacks the honor of God.

The Apostle James confirms this position of the Apostle Paul. In the third chapter of his book he says,

> "But the tongue can no man tame; it is an unruly evil, full of deadly poison. Therewith, bless we God, even the Father; and therewith curse we men, which are made after the similitude (likeness or image) of God. Out of the same mouth proceeds blessing and cursing. My brethren, these things ought not so to be" (James 3:8-10).

God's directive then tells us that we should treat one another with the respect which He has given to us.

The Dignity of the Elderly Highlighted in the Bible

Undoubtedly, the Scriptures afford honor to all people. God respects no one, and, yet, He respects all people because He has created them in His own image. From a biblical perspective, human dignity has always been important, particularly the respect of the elderly. While modern culture looks upon the patriarchal system with suspicion, a system where the elderly apparently controlled the family, a look at the patriarchal system from another vantage point reveals the great dignity with which people treated the elderly.

The Old Testament story of Joseph's treatment of his malevolent brothers, his bringing of his father to Egypt, his provision for all of them, and the establishing of them in the Land of Goshen provides us with a great example of human dignity. It also represents a picture of the patriarchal system at its best. Here we see Jacob give the blessing as a guide for the family. We also see here the patriarch's final request fulfilled -- dignity to the grave (Genesis 46-50).

When we turn to the New Testament, our information becomes more limited by way of family examples. Yet, the fifth chapter of Timothy certainly speaks to human respect. We find here at least three instructions for human relationships which emphasize honor for one another. These include interpersonal relationships (1 Timothy 5:1-2), treatment of widows (1 Timothy 5:3-16), and treatment of the leadership (1 Timothy 5:17-20).

Paul selected the ideal family relationships to instruct us regarding the treatment of all others. He says, in effect, "think of the very best human examples of *fila* or family relationships and let them serve as the standard for all other relationships." Note in particular that we should not rebuke an older person, but instead entreat him as a father (1 Timothy 5:1). Thus, we ought to treat all older people with the same dignity we see expressed in the very best example of child-father relationships.

The instruction of the Apostle regarding widows guards their dignity. Widows first need to provide for themselves or remarry. If widows are unable to provide for themselves or do not remarry, they are to be aided by family. Finally, widows are to be aided by the church. Consider this sequence. It conserves the individual's dignity to "create" and "have dominion" as long as possible. The first line of assistance comes from family, where *fila* love provides a context for caring. Finally, the widow's dignity is protected by receiving assistance from the church when she and her family are no longer able to provide for her needs. At this point, the Christian church family has the responsibility of love to care for those unable to care for themselves.

Dignity and Housing for the Elderly

We find all of the above discussion important to a Christian view of housing for the elderly. The ability to care for yourself, to provide for yourself, and to remain in your own chosen environment affects your sense of dignity. Although Chapter 10 develops the issue of caring for family members, here we will explore the consideration of housing goals and options for the elderly.

Nearly every American family will face these issues at least once during the next 50 years. Many will experience the agony of interdicting their parents' living arrangements only to face the same issues as the elderly parents in 20 or 30 years.

What should be the Christian goal in housing for the elderly? How do we best preserve dignity? Undoubtedly, we have not yet reached unanimity on this matter. However, it seems in accord with human dignity that senior adults should have the opportunity of living in the homes of their choice for as long as possible.

The following diagram attempts to present a flow chart of housing needs for senior citizens:

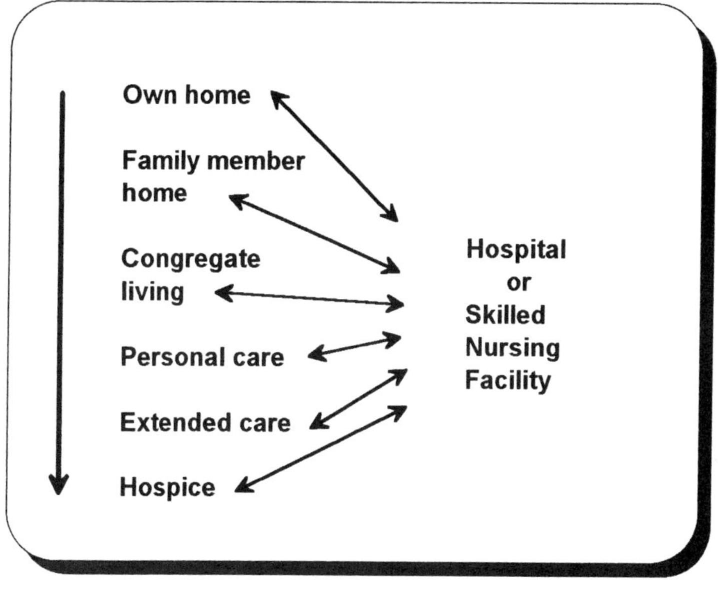

Orderly progression through the levels of housing and care does not necessarily represent the norm. Our flow chart seems to assume a progressive, orderly deterioration. Yet, an individual may go from his own home to extended care, or from a family member's home to hospice care. Often, the hospital or skilled nursing facility is the interim stop between changes in housing requirements. Many times an acute or chronic condition will necessitate a hospital stay, and the individual's needs may require a different level of care upon release from the medical facility. The understanding of this flow chart depends upon some definitions. Let's explore the various terms used in this chart.

Own Home: This term does not exclusively refer to the ownership of the family home, but to the domicile of one's choosing. It may take the form of a home, an apartment, a condominium, or even personal quarters in a congregate living situation.

Family Member: This refers to living in the residence of a family member. This can take the form of an in-law suite, with an independent living arrangement, or a personal room while sharing other family space. The elder's care and supervision are provided within the context of the family and within the capability of the caretakers.

Congregate Living: This refers to living within a complex dedicated to senior adults. The degree of dependency is progressive. It can vary from simply living in the unit to total nursing care. Some congregate living units simply provide living quarters with no dining facilities or medical support.

Personal Care Unit: This is the next step in dependent care. Typically, this living arrangement becomes an option when a person's health has reached the point that he or she forgets medicines, forgets to turn off the stove, or to care for one's own personal needs. The individual can no longer provide meals for himself or herself, change the linens, or clean the living area. At this point, family care could be very appropriate, but not always possible.

A personal care unit is halfway between a congregate living

situation and an extended care situation. Personal care is often best for a person who is mobile. Some elders in personal care even continue to drive a car. A very independent lifestyle is possible, but it is monitored for health and safety reasons.

Extended Care: This is often called the nursing home stage. At this point, the individual can no longer take care of his or her own basic needs. Frequently the individual is bedridden and requires twenty-four hour care. The person does not have access to leave. If properly operated, the extended care nursing facility still offers a place of dignity. In fact, it should ensure self-respect by providing necessary bodily care and providing meaningful activities within the scope of each individual's diminishing abilities.

Hospice Care: Hospice does not necessarily mean a place of care but a type of care. The concept focuses upon caring for the whole person (physical, mental, emotional, and spiritual) at every level of care needed. Hospice care is often provided for individuals who are in the process of dying. This care may be provided in the home or in a nursing facility. Caring for the whole person should always be our goal. (For further information on hospice care for the elderly see Appendix A.)

Conclusion

Dignity is a gift from our Creator. We have no right to take it from one another, yet we also have a responsibility to ensure the maintenance of each other's dignity by the way we treat one another. Few things can disenfranchise someone more quickly than removing the ability to choose one's place of dwelling. We can even extend dignity over a longer period of time by developing a wider spectrum of housing possibilities. The church and its many denominations should give serious consideration to expanding its ministries for elders and their families. The church should include education about its services as part of its ministry. Developing and coordinating services which help senior adults remain in their choice of housing, should also be a part of the church's ministry

The Christian Advocate Ministry (CAM)[5] continues to develop a whole range of services which will facilitate the aging adult to remain in the residence of choice until physical incapacitation demands a move to the next level of care. At that point, CAM will provide assistance in the transition to the next necessary level of care.

10

HOME, WHERE ASSISTED CARE BEGINS

My son was two years old when my parents moved into the in-law suite in our home. My father and mother both found it difficult to leave the parenting to us. My father was a caring man, but was also negative much of the time. This negative attitude and his regular incursion into the discipline of my children, especially my son, provoked periodic painful experiences for the entire family. These conditions presented my son with unwanted opportunities for growth. After five years my mother died and my father soon became more closely integrated into our family. His mental capacities diminished rapidly, and he was finally diagnosed with Alzheimer's disease.

During this time, with increasing regularity, my son watched me playing the role of parent to my father. I remember sitting down with my son on a number of occasions to explain these confusing dynamics to him. Quite often, the thoughts of my own aging would haunt me. "Remember, your day is coming." Then, I would remember that paraphrase of our Lord's words, "Do unto others as you would have them do unto you" (Matthew 7:12). This thought would trigger a prayer. "Lord," I would pray, "give me the grace to treat Dad in a way that pleases you. Help me to treat him the way I would want him to treat me. My son is watching me. Help me to be a good example of love to him. Help him to learn how love operates in a tough situation."

I struggled at times. However, an encouraging incident occurred prior to my father's death when I knew that the Lord was assuring me that my overall treatment of my Dad had been a debt of love. It happened one day as I was drying him after his bath. He had one of those lucid moments, characteristic of an Alzheimer's mind. He looked at me with tears in his eye. He called me by his longtime name of affection for me. "Kid," he said, "I'd be in an awful fix if it were not for you. Thank you." The blank stare then returned to his eyes. I am grateful for that affirmation and that tender moment.

The home of children, and sometimes other relatives, frequently is, and should be the first place of extended or assisted care. Home refers to the place of love-bonds and familiarity. It also provides an opportunity for spiritual growth and human maturing. Obviously, the family can exercise its biblical responsibility to care for its own in such a warm environment, but with economic restraint in mind.

Caring for an aging relative in your home requires planning, preparation, and regular staff meetings. The family will serve as much better providers if they function together as a staff. They will function better if they think and act as a staff.

In addition, planning is important to the success of any enterprise. Unfortunately, taking on the care of a relative too often just happens. A crisis precipitates action. While we make some quick preparations, like moving a child and his belongings in with a sibling to provide a room, we often overlook more serious planning.

What kind of planning is imperative? The breadth of the planning depends somewhat upon the circumstances. Yet, we still need to consider certain matters and ask key questions as well, such as:

1. What long-term effects can we expect from this action? About how long will the relative stay? Will the relative be able to return to his/her own residence? Will one member of the family need to terminate employment to provide the care?

2. What short-term effects can we expect from this action? How much disruption in the family routine will occur? Will a college-aged child need to postpone school for a semester to provide help? Will any of the children have to give up a bedroom, or will the family need to give up

the recreation room?

3. Regarding physical planning, will we need to or want to add on to the house? If so, who will finance it? If the parent will finance it, what kind of legal agreement should we use to ensure that misunderstandings do not occur? Will we need to make modifications to the home (wheelchair entrance, etc.)? Will we need to purchase another vehicle?

4. Regarding relationship planning, we need to consider three areas of concern.

   The first focuses upon the marriage of the adult children caregivers. Remember, marriage represents God's basic unit of society. If it falters, the family falters. A couple will have to think carefully about the additional demands of caregiving. How will they maintain their relationship? How will they gain respite so that they will still have time for some church fellowship and fun together? How will they provide for private time? Will the caregivers have sufficient rest time to maintain their energies and composure under stress?

   The second area of concern emphasizes family life. How can mother and father have time together with the children? What about family outings and vacations? What about family traditions and relationships with the spouse's family?

   Relationships with and between the children presents the third area of concern. Will the children have to be quiet all the time? Can the children have normal friendships, with their friends being allowed to come into the house? Who will be the parent? Will the grandparent refrain from interfering in the discipline of the children? We knew going into our situation that this would present a problem area. It proved to be greater than we had planned. (Had our analysis been more accurate when my parents moved into our family home, certain modifications to our home would have been helpful.) What effect will a chronically ill grandparent have on the child? How will you explain the possible eventual death of the relative in the home to the children?

5. Another troublesome component of caring for a relative concerns that of authority. Have the prospective caregivers become sufficiently independent of the parent(s)? That is, has the couple achieved the biblical mandate to "leave their parents and cleave to one another?" If this question is answered in the negative, the caregivers will have great difficulty maintaining control of their own home. Is the relative willing to be cooperative? Or, will this person attempt to manipulate the caregivers and precipitate power struggles?

Some of these questions are unpleasant to raise and even more vexing to face. Yet, if you do not give them a credible hearing in the planning stage, they will haunt the caregiver's home and mind.

Moreover, problems which surface during this planning stage should not automatically dictate a decision not to care for a relative. Remember, no family can become a caregiving family without having to face some adjustments. Adjustments bring stress for everyone. On the other hand, they also bring opportunity for growth to adults and children alike (Romans 5:3-6; James 1:2-5). The question is not, "Will there be stress?" but rather "Is our family capable of handling the stress?" If not, the family should seriously reevaluate this decision to care for an elderly relative. The question might also arise, "Are there physical or circumstantial limitations which restrict our caring for this person?" If the answer is affirmative, then you must seek a suitable alternative.

The preparation phase should also produce a prayerfully devised process to mitigate the anticipated difficulties. Take the time to answer each question raised in the planning phase. You must adopt an effective approach in which to address each issue. You may find it wise to secure a notebook and entitle it *Our Family*

Caregiving Plan. A written record of each problem issue and a clear summary of the actions needed become essential for addressing these problems systematically. Once you have created this action plan, then you are ready to begin preparation for bringing your elderly relative into your home.

Preparation may include sitting down with the children to discuss what to expect. If one child must give up his or her room and will now share a room with a sibling, then you must help the children work through this change. This is also a good time to teach them about the sacrifice of giving, the cost of discipleship, and the giving nature of love (1 Corinthians 13:4-8; John 3:16-18).

If modifications to the home become necessary, you may find it better to work out a short stay in a nursing home or other facility for the parent during these preparations. I do not advise starting the caregiving adventure while facing a set of circumstances which compounds the stress.

Even though you may have circumstantial, economic, and social pressures to move quickly, it is better not to make this move without the planning and preparation phases in place. A caregiving experience bathed in prayer, planning, and preparation reduces confusion and frustration which result from foolish haste.

Mary has cared for her 85-year-old mother, Rose, for three-and-one-half years. She and Mike have managed a one-week vacation each year and several one-day outings together through a county-sponsored respite service. They have not been able to do any activities with the children at all. One Saturday a month, Mike cares for Rose so that Mary can spend the day with the children. School activities have resulted in a one-parent-only affair since Rose came to live with them.

Recently, Mary went to the doctor with chest pains. "Stress" was the doctor's one firm word, accompanied by a lecture. Mike reluctantly shared with Mary his own struggles with jealousy over Rose's increasing demands on Mary as well as the demands of her deteriorating body.

The first three years of caring for Rose seemed to work out well. Then, Rose's bladder control failed. She began to act unkind to Mary and the children. She also refused to wear a diaper and restricted herself to the bed. Her clear mind became clouded with resentment, and her pleasant disposition evolved into depression. She even refused to talk with the pastor.

Mike finally called an "emergency staff meeting" after the report from the doctor. Mary, Mike, and the three children (ages 12, 11 and 9) all gathered around the table to talk. After prayer, Mike declared that the family had reached its limits and that other arrangements for Rose needed to be made as a result.

How should this family proceed? How can a family recognize when the time has come to terminate in-home caregiving for an aging relative? I have provided some principles to help answer this question. Apply them to Mike and Mary, and see if you think they have reached the transfer point for Rose. Has a nursing home become the best way to pay the debt of love both to Rose and each other in the family? The Scripture from which these principles logically arise is Romans 13:8.

Principle #1: It is time to terminate in-home care when we become inadequate to provide care.

The inadequacy may arise for various reasons. Perhaps, the primary caregiver no longer can physically provide the care needed. Or, maybe the caregiver has exhausted the outside support systems which have enabled him/her to function. Furthermore, the caregiver may not have the emotional stamina to continue to offer the necessary care. Perhaps a more demanding level of care is now needed. A change in employment may now make continued care impossible.

Principle #2: It is time to terminate in-home caregiving when the recipient is no longer able to profit from the care.

Always remember that love does what is best for our loved ones, not ourselves. When the relative no longer profits from the care received at home, it is time for the caregiver to relinquish his role. For any number of reasons, caregivers often become caregivers, not so much out of love for the needy person, but to fulfill some need of their own. Such motivation is not paying the debt of love.

Principle #3: It is time to terminate in-home caregiving when the recipient's desires are inconsistent with his/her needs.

Frequently, parents attempt to extract promises from children to never put them into a nursing home. In light of the conditions of some nursing homes, it is little wonder that they may go to extreme lengths to ensure that their children will not place them in one of "those places!" My father often repeated this demand to me, but my answer always remained the same.

"Dad, as long as I can care for you in a proper manner, I'll not place you in a nursing home."

We can see this love played out in the life and ministry of Jesus Christ. He did not immediately give the care to people that they desired and often not in the way they desired it. He provided care for them in a manner consistent with their spiritual needs. One person Jesus healed immediately by touch, sending him off whole and instructing him how to grow spiritually from the experience. In another case, He used an indirect means of providing healing in order that His care for the spiritual needs of that person might have its greatest effect, both upon the individual and his world. His care consistently met the needs of the person, not just his or her desires. This represents true love.

To state this principle another way, it is not necessarily what our elder wants, but what they need that must be provided. When 24-hour medical care or constant physical care is indicated, then a nursing home may well provide what is needed. Manipulations, guilt trips, and anger notwithstanding, we must then pass the baton of care off to another.

These three principles, well marinated with Romans 13:8, can comprise the litmus test for terminating home care and initiating nursing home care.

11

THE NURSING HOME NECESSITY

Twenty-five million people aged 65 or older lived in America in 1980. That represented 11 percent of the population. By the year 2030, the projection for people 65 or older is about 55 million, or 22 percent of the total number of people in the United States. At the present time, people aged 80 or more comprise the fastest growing segment of the population. Between 1980 and 2000, predictions show an expected increase of 67 percent in this age group. Approximately 63 percent of this group also experience some degree of functional disability. At the rate of the current trends, the numbers of people in nursing homes will increase by approximately 50 percent in 20 years and 100 percent in 50 years. The average nursing home resident is between 78 and 82 years of age, white, female, widowed or never married, and suffering from multiple chronic health conditions.

This growing number of aging Americans precipitates the "nursing home necessity." The primary caregiver is usually a female member of the family. With the increasing number of working women, clearly this resource of caregivers has decreased. How else can America, and Christians in particular, meet this escalating demand? Is it the Christian's responsibility to care for aging parents? What about the aging uncle or aunt who had no children and whose immediate family is no longer living or declines to exercise sufficient care for them?

No one likes to face these possibilities, but the statistics leave little doubt that many Christian Americans will encounter the necessity of caring for an older family member. In this chapter, we will discuss biblical principles which impinge upon how we should negotiate this life contingency.

The following situation involving Frank and Mary is not typical. However, we present it in order to illustrate the biblical principles that can guide people through the most difficult predicaments.

Frank's parents are in their early 80's. His mother is confined to a wheelchair, and his father is partially blind. They have lived with Frank and his family for the past seven years in a comfortable arrangement. Recently, his father's health has deteriorated significantly. He has been hospitalized twice and has required special care upon returning home. Frank's mother has begun to experience regular loss of bladder control.

On the day that Frank's father came home from the hospital, his mother-in-law suffered a stroke and was hospitalized. Yesterday, Frank and Mary were informed that Mary's mother does not qualify for government assistance with nursing home costs after the first 14 days since she is medically able to return home. Mary's father, however, is in such poor health that he cannot care for his wife.

To complicate matters further, Mary's uncle, while in good health, has lost much of his rational capacities. Consequently, he needs to live with someone who will supervise his medication as well as his daily life routine. However, he has no children and no family, other than Frank and Mary.

Obviously, Frank and Mary need assistance. Quite possibly, a nursing home has also become a necessity at this point in time. As you read through the suggested principles, ask yourself how you would apply them if you were in Frank and Mary's place.

Biblical Principles For Sorting Out Responsibilities

1. **Caring.** I am my brother's keeper (Genesis 4:8-10). As believers, we have a responsibility to look after the welfare of our brother (a parent or older relative in this case). At times we may delegate that responsibility, but we cannot disavow it.

2. **Compassion.** Inasmuch as you have done it to the least of one of these, you will be rewarded (Matthew 25:34-46). Compassion is a hallmark of Christianity. A visit to a nursing home, particularly to the floor where care is provided for

the feeble-minded, will generate some emotion for most people. While the overriding emotion is compassion, many will also feel disgust. The heart of the visitor to the nursing home fills with a desire to bring something better to the people observed. As Christians, we must be compassionate and determine just what we can do for this person living in the nursing home.

3. **Concern.** In James 1:26-27, a verb is used that is translated as "visit" into our English versions. The word, however, carries the meaning of intent. The possessor of true religion does not just pay the widow a friendly visit. He visits with the intent of helping in whatever way needed. The word also occurs in an infinitive form, which expresses purpose. Kistemaker observes, "Social conditions in ancient times were such that orphans and widows were unproted (unprovided for) because they had no guardian (caregiver) and breadwinner. If one has true religion, he will express concern by providing for legitimate needs."[6]

4. **Love**. (Romans 13:8). Within the family of God, love is the prevailing characteristic. God, our Father, represents love. He has set the example for us to follow, even in the social realm. "For God so loved that He gave..." illustrates the grandest example possible. However, God also gives us some clear directives about love (Psalms 68:5; 146:9; Deuteronomy 10:18; and Matthew 6:32). We clearly see from the Word that God expects His children to imitate Him in showing love. (See also Deuteronomy 14:29; Ezekiel 22:7; and Acts 6:1-6).

5. **Leave and Cleave**. In the institution of marriage, God lays down the "divide and absorb" principle of marriage. A man leaves his father and mother and cleaves to his wife. He and his wife divide from their families of origin and become absorbed in each other to create a new family unit. This joining together presents to us a principle that we must not violate, even though the care of elderly parents may impinge upon it. Caregiving must flow from the cleaving of a couple, not from

the diluting or dissolving of the couple.

6. **Financial responsibility** falls to children before parents (Proverbs 13:22). The care of children, including education, takes precedence over caring for parents. Children do not displace parents, but caring for parents must not prevent the accomplishment of caring for one's children.

7. **Spiritual dedication of financial resources** does not alleviate the responsibility of caring for one's parents (Mark 7:11, Berkley Version). This passage clearly shows us that the Lord will not be pleased with such a spiritual shame.

What Constitutes A Nursing Home Necessity?

Most people would look at the situation mentioned earlier and conclude that a nursing home is a necessity for Frank's family. However, the nursing home necessity may arise in much less severe circumstances.

Some older adults may even reach the place where they can no longer live alone and may actually find it more comfortable in a nursing home. The social interaction, organized activities, and peer group companionship may all contribute to the life satisfaction of some older adults more than living with their family. For those of us who have had pleasant family relationships, this seems incredulous. However, for families who have had conflict-ridden or distant relationships, such an arrangement may be very satisfactory. In addition, some older adults simply prefer to be with peers. Furthermore, a family may provide housing, medication management, and general oversight but the demands on each of its members may preclude sufficient time for a daily game of checkers, lingering conversation, or any form of companionship from 8:00 A.M. until after work hours. Given a choice, the older adult may prefer congregate living.

Each family will have to decide for itself when a nursing home has become a necessity. This is usually a decision that you should make in consultation with several professional providers. Depending upon the case, the following individuals should be part of the consulting team: the older adult (if mental capacity allows), the older adult's physician, a social worker, a local government agent who may assist with placement and financial arrangements, and last, but not least, the minister. The burden of responsibility to assemble this team will most often fall upon the next of kin. In the case of hospital discharge, the hospital social worker will frequently expedite placement.

Choosing A Nursing Home

How do you determine which nursing home to utilize? In some instances, you will not have a choice. This is true for several reasons. First, there may be very little availability. In addition, some communities do not have sufficient nursing home space. You may also face financial constraints. Nursing homes are expensive. They range from approximately $1,400 to $3,400 per month. Some will take public-assisted residents, but some will not. Distance from family may limit choices as well.

Some suggestions for choosing a nursing home include the following:

1. Visit a variety of homes. After you have collected the data from each home, create a report card for yourself and grade each home visited.

    a. Decide ahead of time the services desired. Take the literature given at each home and organize it so that you can compare "apples to apples."

    b. Decide what aspects of a nursing home are important to you and your resident family member.

    c. Interview several workers (even a maid). Ask how they like working at the facility and with the elderly. The National Institute on Aging (NIA) shows that workers who like the elderly contribute to the improvement of elderly attitudes and conditions.

2. Review the nursing home's state inspection records available at the home itself, at the Social Security Office, or from the Department of Social Services.

3. Read the contract very closely. You may even want to have an attorney review it.

4. Contact the Department of Social Services for financial information and assistance.

Developing A Care Plan

When a loved one moves to a nursing home, the family still has a responsibility to that person. You need to remember three important points as this transition takes place. First, remember that the nursing home may not, and in some cases does not, take complete care of your loved one. Presuming you have considered these matters in making the choice of a home, discuss them again when your loved one actually becomes a resident. Find out just what you can do and what the home allows or provides. Remember that companionship is a high priority. Review the biblical principles discussed earlier in this chapter and ask yourself how these are included in your care plan. People appreciate the personal touch. I remember one story about a woman who went by the nursing home each day on the way to work and spent fifteen minutes brushing her mother's long hair. The mother could no longer raise her arms to do this task and the nurses simply pulled her hair back. This loving attention to a small detail brought praise for her daughter whenever someone visited the mother.

Second, focus on quality. You cannot do everything you would like to do or that needs to be done, so what you are able to do should be of high quality. The story above illustrates this point. Brushing her mother's hair was a high quality action by the daughter because it meant so much to her mother.

Finally, be realistic about your time. I have spoken with

many people who live under a constant sense of guilt. They have set goals for a care plan which, given their time restraints, was impossible to follow. Yet, they judged themselves by these goals and always came up wanting. This condition robs the caregiver of the joy of caring. It also disturbs one's relationships with the Lord and their elderly loved one. The Lord only gives each of us 24 hours in a day. Most likely, one of the reasons your loved one lives in the nursing home is because you and your family did not have the time to care for him or her at home.

Developing A Personal Care Plan

Caregivers must observe the three "R's." This is true whether caring for someone at home or someone in a nursing home. The first "R" refers to **relaxation**. A caregiver cannot cease to live his or her own life. Activities which have played a part in one's life routine, like playing tennis on Tuesday and Thursday after work, need to continue. An occasional departure is normal, but relaxation cannot become lax. Part of relaxation means companionship for oneself. Don't lose friendships in the crunch of carrying out a care plan for your loved one.

The second "R" stands for **refreshment**. You need regular spiritual input into your life. Do not give up church attendance to spend time at the nursing home. An occasional weekend missed from your care plan in order to go on a retreat or to spend time with your spouse provides a necessary aspect of your own refreshment. Remember that even Jesus retreated from His care for the disciples and for the people in general once in awhile.

The third "R" focuses on **reassurance**. Review your care plan periodically and evaluate its effectiveness in caring for your loved one and its effect upon you and your family. Remember that God does not expect you to be a superman or superwoman.

Tool for Self Evaluation

At some point in life, a nursing home may become a real

possibility for yourself or a loved one. As this choice becomes a reality, individuals may benefit from exploring their own attitudes about nursing homes. To be prepared for this type of transition, we need to identify areas where one's attitude may indicate the probability of conflict with the person going into a nursing home, family members making the nursing home decision, or with nursing home employees. We include the following tool to help you think through your own ideas about the pros and cons of utilizing nursing home care. You should seek to discuss your answers with your pastor or with a qualified counselor. Families may also wish to take this inventory separately for use as a discussion tool when the nursing home has become a necessity.

FAMILY MEMBER SELF-INVENTORY

Section I

Please place a "T" (true) or "F" (false) before each statement.

My perceptions of a nursing home have included the following:

_____ 1. A warehouse for old people.
_____ 2. A service for fee extended to families to enable them to provide the care they can no longer give.
_____ 3. Characterized by unclean conditions.
_____ 4. A place to live as fully as possible despite diminishing abilities.
_____ 5. Heavy use of medication to keep residents quiet.
_____ 6. Bland, poor quality food.
_____ 7. Minimal care provided by marginal employees.
_____ 8. A place where planned programs encourage and enhance social contact.
_____ 9. Characterized by nutritious meals planned for elderly physiological needs.
_____ 10. Extended hospital care in a hospital-like setting.
_____ 11. Characterized by bland decor.

Section II

This questionnaire was devised for use after the entrance processing of a family member to a nursing home. If you have not experienced this processing with your family member, skip the questions that are meaningless to you, and answer the remainder of the questions in terms of your relationship with your elderly family member. Please place an "X" before as many statements under each entry that apply to you.

12. When we discussed patient rights, I was impressed with:

_____ The legislative concern with my relative's rights.

_____ The responsibility placed upon family for resident care.

_____ The extent to which one patient's rights could impinge on another patient's rights.

13. I would characterize my relationship with my relative as:

_____ Warm and affectionate.

_____ Distant and caring.

_____ Strained.

_____ Deteriorating.

_____ A responsibility.

14. I understand that Family Council means:

_____ A nursing home organization run by the staff.

_____ A private membership organization.

_____ A resident-run program.

_____ A family member-run organization.

_____ A volunteer-run organization for the benefit of residents and their families.

15. I understand the purpose(s) of Family Council to be:

_____ A sort of "group therapy" session for family members.

_____ An educational organization.

_____ An organization to provide a forum for communication between family and staff.

_____ An organization of family members to provide services to residents.

16. Family Council strikes me as:

_____ One more activity to demand my time.

_____ Another occasion for me to feel guilty because I cannot or do not want to participate.

_____ A useful tool to enhance communication between

staff and families.

_____ A useful tool to promote communication between family members.

17. I am inclined to attend Family Council for the following reason(s):

_____ I want to know what is going on at the facility.
_____ I want to have access to the facility management.
_____ I want to support the staff and other families.
_____ I anticipate the need for support from other family members.

18. I am inclined **not** to attend Family Council for the following reason(s):

_____ I am a private person.
_____ I think the staff is competent and trust their judgment.
_____ I have too many other responsibilities.
_____ It would be too painful for me to engage in conversation about my relative in the facility context.

19. Private pay residents should:

_____ Receive preferential treatment.
_____ Be treated on an equal basis with government-assisted residents.
_____ Be in a separate wing of the facility.
_____ None of the above.

20. I would appreciate help with visiting my elderly relative in the following areas:

_____ Appropriate topics of discussion.
_____ Appropriate activities to attempt.
_____ The value of visitation in light of my relative's condition.

_____ None of the above.

21. At the time of admission, I experienced the following:

_____ A sense of relief.
_____ A sense of relief accompanied by guilt for feeling relieved.
_____ Guilt for placing my relative in the facility.
_____ Fear of what effect the placement will have on my relative.

Section III

If you have not placed your family member in a nursing home, please answer these questions with the prospect of a nursing home placement in view. Research and experience indicate that people placing a family member in a nursing home endure some of the following emotions. These are normal. Mark with an "X" the following statements which apply to you.

_____ 22. I feel guilty for placing my relative in the facility.

_____ 23. I feel angry at my relative because I had to admit him/her to a nursing home.

_____ 24. I feel angry toward other family members who are not helping me with this task.

_____ 25. I feel guilty because I could not keep my relative at home.

_____ 26. I am fearful that my relative will be unhappy in the facility.

_____ 27. I am fearful that my relative will lose his/her dignity.

_____ 28. I feel angry because of the burden of managing my relative's estate.

_____ 29. I struggle with resentment over the depletion of my relative's estate.

_____ 30. I am concerned that my relative will become inactive.

_____ 31. I am concerned that my relative's funds will be depleted before his death because our family cannot afford to pay for his care.

_____ 32. I vacillate between resentment and guilt over the demand of visiting my relative.

Section IV

If your family member is not yet in a nursing home, please skip questions 33-35 and answer the remainder of the questions in terms of your anticipation of your family member's move to a nursing home. Please fill in the blanks or complete the question with a brief statement or discussion.

33. The following describes my perceptions of visitation in the facility:

    a. I should visit my relative _____ times per week.
    b. My visits should be _____ hours in length.
    c. The following people should visit this relative at least weekly:

    ____

    ____.

34. I should feel free to assist the staff when I am visiting by,

    ____

    ____.

35. In the short time my relative has been a resident, I have found my visits to be:

    a. A __________ experience because ________________
    ____.

    b. Visitation seems to be ____________ since my relative
    ____.

36. What is your greatest concern for your relative who has become a resident in this facility?

    ____
    ____.

37. What do you understand least about the functions of this facility?

    ____
    ____.

38. What things in your contact with the nursing home did you find offensive?

    ____
    ____.

39. Which of your relative's needs are most important to you?

    ____
    ____.

40. What, if anything, have you seen in this facility that has bothered you? ____________________________________
    ____.

41. Does any other issue irritate you?

    ____
    ____
    ____.

12

CAESAR, ME AND AGING

George retired at age 65. It took Jim, his son, several months to convince George that receiving Social Security would not violate his Christian convictions. Jim sat down with his father and worked out, at length, his contributions to the system and the accumulated value of compound interest in order to help George see that he had, in fact, created the funds which he could now withdraw. George finally agreed that he could draw Social Security, at least until he had exhausted his contributions.

George and Jim are fictitious people. However, George represents the attitude of some Christians toward government programs for the elderly. "We are to be dependent upon God and not Caesar!" To receive assistance from the social system means a failure to exercise faith in God for His provision.

Is such an attitude valid? What relationship should aging Christians sustain to government programs? Is faith in God's provision circumscribed when government assistance is accepted? These present real issues for us to consider. For example, when someone is ordained to the ministry, he or she has the option, as a conscientious objector, to opt out of the Social Security system. The question of conscience becomes significant enough as the system provides this window of opportunity based upon religious convictions. Therefore, contemplate the following principles from Romans 13:1-7 when considering whether it is appropriate to use governmental resources in assisting an elderly person.

Principle #1: Distinction of the many relationships of the Christian (Romans 13:1-7).

James Stifler offers helpful insight into the principle that Christians have several distinct, but God-ordained relationships.[7] He writes in *The Epistle To The Romans* that the Christian sustains some relationships which are purely spiritual in nature and some which are natural relationships. Spiritual relationships have Christ the Redeemer as their source, and natural relationships have God the Creator as their source.

First, the Christian has a responsibility to and a relationship with his Savior, Jesus Christ. Secondly, the Christian is to be in relationship with the church. It is not necessary here to spend a great amount of time detailing these two relationships. However, historically Christians have confused their relationship to the church with their third area of relationship. This last area for consideration is the Christian's relationship to the state. Because of this confusion, we will focus on explaining how the Christian must look at his or her relationship with the state or government.

Since the Christian is told in the Bible to have a submissive relationship with Jesus, the church and the government, it is important to remember that all three of these distinct types of relationships are ordained by God in His Word. God has established the power of the state and being in relationship with God does not invalidate being in relationship with both the church and the government.

In other words, as a creature of God, we sustain a "creaturely" relationship with God. But, as Christians, we also sustain a fila (redemptive) relationship with God. Principle 1, which states that the Christian has several distinct relationships, grows out of the fact that we are both citizens of the church and of the state. God ordains both, and neither invalidates the other.

Principle #2: Subjection to the state is incumbent upon the Christian (Romans 13:1- 5).

Paul affirms this principle twice in this passage. He introduces his subject with, "Let every soul be subject unto the higher powers" (Romans 13:1a). In verse 5, Paul reiterates this thought when he says, "You must be subject. . . ."

John Calvin's observation makes this principle clear.

> "He [Paul] calls them [the governing officials] higher powers, because they excel other men, rather than supreme, as though they possess the highest authority. Magistrates, therefore, are so called in relation to those who are subject to them, and not from any comparison between them. By using this expression, Paul intended, I think, to remove the empty curiosity of those who often ask by what right those who are in authority came by their power. It ought really to be sufficient for us that they rule. They have not attained this high position by their own strength, but have been placed there by the hand of the Lord. By mentioning every soul, Paul removes every exception, lest any should claim to be immune from the common submission to obedience".[8]

Calvin had no doubt that Paul held all men responsible to be subject to the state.

Principle #3: Government is established by God for good (Romans 13:3-4).

It seems that Paul speaks of good in three ways. First of all, he uses "good" to describe the kind of works which government does not oppose. The word which Paul uses here is a wide ranging word and is certainly able to be inclusive of modern day social programs.

Secondly, Paul observes that the government applauds those who themselves do good. Paul also indicates that the state encourages the development of good works. Again, the concept is inclusive enough to encompass social assistance programs. In our society, this may take the form of the federal government awarding block grants through various private agencies to fund programs (good works) which they have designed.

The third observation regarding Paul's use of the word "good" is this. He considers the government to be "the minister of good" to the Christian. Paul says, "For he (the state official) is the minister of God to you for good." This rather strongly asserts God's intention for the state. Calvin again writes:

> "Magistrates may learn from this [the fact that God ordained the magistrate's authority] the nature of their calling. They are not to rule on their own account, but for the public good. Nor do they have unbridled power, but power that is restricted to the welfare of their subjects. In short, they are responsible to God and to men in the exercise of their rule. Since they have been chosen by God and do His business, they are answerable to Him. But the ministry which God has committed to them has reference to their subjects. They have also therefore an obligation to them. Paul instructs individuals that it is by the divine kindness that they are defended by the sword of rulers against the injuries of the wicked".[9]

While neither of the governments over Paul or Calvin had developed significant social programs, it seems to be clear to us that "the minister of God to you for good" has evolved in modern society to include a diversity of assistance programs for a variety of needs. We can also clearly see that a passage like this has given impetus to the social implications of the Gospel. Notice that it did not give rise to the "social gospel." Nevertheless, the Christian attitude toward government, the influence of a "mega-segment" of society of Christians, and the resulting interaction between the Christian's relationships in the redemptive and the creative spheres has produced a Western society in which the state has become, in a broad sense, "the minister to you for good." We must see this advancement as the consequence of Christianity. While we cannot assume that this condition will continue, we still have a good reason to participate in its benefits.

Principle #4: That for which you pay taxes is
that to which you are entitled (Romans 13:6-7).

God established government for the purposes discussed above.

God instructs Christians to pay taxes ("Render unto Caesar the things which are Caesar's; and unto God the things that are God's; Matthew 22:21). Therefore, when Christians receive services from state agencies, they participate according to how much they have contributed. God established government to do good, and government collects taxes to do good. Accessing the good offered means to capitalize on the system which God has put in place.

Some will argue that Romans 13:6-7 only deals with maintaining peace and punishing evil. However, we should also remember that Rome had a sophisticated system of services. One such model to observe concerns Paul, who claimed his right to Roman citizenship, a good ministered by the state, and utilized it for his own welfare.

Overview of Government Delivery System of Services for Aging

The following diagram presents an overview of the government's delivery system of services for the aging. The flow chart does not account for all existing services at the federal, state, or local levels. However, you can usually obtain additional information on other available services through the office of the Area Agency on Aging.

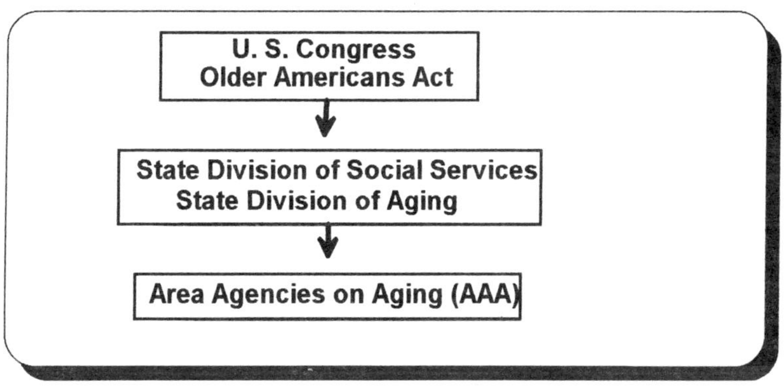

Working through the government may, at times, be a complicated, frustrating process. With new legislation passed every year, the services available to assist the family often change. Only a tenacious approach to determining what services are available, and how to apply for them, brings forth the needed help. Despite the difficulties encountered in understanding and utilizing government resources, our country has provided one of the most extensive, comprehensive, and usable systems in the entire world.

For more information about government resources available to the elderly, see Chapter 16, "Caregiver's Directory of Resources."

Conclusion

At the very least, we can note that the principles studied in this chapter make it difficult for Christians to reject out-of-hand programs of good works devised and administered by the state. All Christians and their families will have to decide for themselves whether or not, in good conscience, they can participate in the benefits of such programs. However, no family should reject such aid without a careful evaluation of the principles suggested in this study.

13

THE ROLE OF COUNSELING IN THE AGING PROCESS

Many older adults who read this book do not belong to a study group where the issues mentioned in the previous chapters are discussed and evaluated. Since this material was originally written with a study group in mind, we found it pertinent to add this chapter for those not in a study group.

Older adults are often skeptical of counseling. It frequently connotes mental illness, not only to older generations, but to younger ones as well. The cartoons appearing in magazines and newspapers often depict those who seek help as foolish and those that counsel as having a god-complex. Unfortunately, too often the puns smack of truth. The fact remains that God often uses skilled helpers to enable us to sort out the complexities of life.

The Bible provides us with an ample theology of counseling.[11] Not only does the Bible provide clear evidence that we should seek counsel, but it also prescribes the responsibility for counseling as a role for every Christian (Romans 15:14; Colossians 3:16; Galatians 6:1-2, 10; and see also a concordance study of key verbs in these passages).

Frequent counseling concerns regarding the aging process include the matters discussed in this chapter. Perhaps you are presently experiencing some of the issues discussed in this book. If so, we trust that this book has helped you. While you may have gained some insight, or a particular bit of knowledge from your reading, I recommend discussing both the problem and what you have learned with your pastor or another competent counselor. These helpers can enable you to weave what you have learned into the fabric of life and can help you to resolve the issues you are facing.

Retirement Planning

The majority of people reaching retirement will have to do their own planning. Only a few companies provide such programs. Most people only think in terms of finances when they consider retirement planning. Charles and Jean are good examples.

Charles planned to have his home paid off by age 62. Between 62 and 65, he planned to do the repairs and replacements necessary to ensure that his home would cost him only taxes and reasonable upkeep for the next 15 years. He then created a retirement account to supplement Social Security and investigated supplemental insurance as well. However, he failed to plan for the use of his time after retirement, necessary adjustments in his marriage, and the productive use of his mind.

Notice, though, that Charles did plan. However, he did not include Jean in the planning process. Little wonder that after Charles retired she was angry and resentful of his sleeping until noon and disgusted "with what he has become in the past year."

Financial planning for retirement is extremely important. The statistical projections of the great number of older adults who will suffer from financial difficulties over the next 25 years is frightening. However, the impact of improper planning for social, religious, intellectual, and physical well-being cannot be underestimated. In fact, good planning in these areas will have a positive impact upon your own financial condition as well.

For example, a gentleman shared with me recently the plan that he and his wife developed. Toward the end of his career, he had the opportunity to be transferred to Florida. Since his wife had a health condition which was predicted to respond well to the climate, they accepted the transfer. At first, they rejected the idea. Their children were all within driving distance of their present home. They wished to see their grandchildren frequently. Such a move would interfere. After further consideration, however, they arrived at a well-defined decision, after considering the following factors:

1. Climate good for wife's health.
2. His hobby is playing and coaching tennis. In Florida, he could do both year-round.
3. Her hobby is gardening. In Florida, she could do this year-round.
4. As a family, they regularly took vacations in Florida, and their children were now doing so with their children. Therefore, a home in Florida could provide a family vacation spot.
5. All three of their children are school teachers. Therefore, they could visit three times a year, plus enjoy an extended stay over the summer.
6. The company would pay for the relocation and absorb their home if it did not sell.
7. Since his business had included consulting work with nursing homes, he would be able to develop some accounts while working for his company to later perform on a contract basis.
8. They have both enjoyed Florida throughout their adult lives.
9. They had developed friends in several cities, and his brother also lived in Florida.
10. Their former pastor now ministers in Tampa and would be a source of long-standing friendship.

As the man shared these things with me, I was impressed with his holistic thinking. His planning included all of the major areas of life.

Marital Adjustment

Many couples have managed to enjoy a reasonably happy marriage during the working years simply because they have maintained limited contact with one another. Retirement frequently increases the time a couple spends together. Poor communication skills, inability to sustain intimacy, and irritations previously glossed over can all become exaggerated in a retirement setting.

A competent Christian counselor can often help the preparation for adjusting a marriage to retirement by providing four to six sessions with the couple. Such sessions may include an assessment of the couple's communication system, their ability to sustain intimacy and their spiritual pilgrimage. Listening and responding to several tape series, reading and interacting through selected books, and completing inventories include only a few of the useful projects which the counselor may assign. Any couple would find such work worthwhile to keep their relationship intact. You should view this procedure like a good all-points auto check before departing on a long trip, or a medical check-up before entering into a vigorous exercise program.

Family Concerns

We have discussed many of these issues in the previous chapters; however, we cannot overstate the need for others to assist us in resolving these problems. While at a meeting a few weeks ago, a pastor shared with me that he had a woman in her mid-30's in his congregation who struggled with the guilt of not going to the nursing home to feed her mother three times a day. He also was aware of the material in the Teacher's Manual of "The Christian Handbook on Aging." Therefore, armed with this material, he visited her and went over this information with her. As a result, she began to resolve her inner conflict.

These family concerns are varied. "How can I get my daughter to discipline her child?" asked a senior adult who lived with her daughter. She was concerned that she would interfere with the family life. "How do I help my mother realize she cannot live alone any longer?" inquired a bright-eyed, optimistic school teacher who respected her mother's desire for independence, but still remained concerned for her safety. "How do I relate to my brothers and sisters, who refuse to help with the burden of caring for Dad?" is a frequent question for those who seek counseling. "How do we enable Dad to face reality about mother's condition?" is another recurrent question. Many of these issues should and do precipitate counseling.

Furthermore, because we are ashamed or unwilling to seek

counseling, issues become crises. However, by the grace of God, many of these crises generate opportunities and possibilities for growth. We wrote this book with the prayer that it will encourage many to face issues before they become crises in the family, but, if a crisis does occur, we pray that you will seek counseling and turn your crisis into an opportunity for personal and spiritual growth.

Health Care Management

We discussed the various phases of health care management in Chapters 8-11. Again, we did not include all contingencies, nor did we consider the individuality of cases. To make wise decisions on medical interventions for an elderly person, you may need to consult a counselor, your pastor, and other persons in the health care system.

You will surely desire to consult your pastor or a Christian counselor when ethical issues arise. In our society, God has seen fit to allow us to encroach upon His domain. With our technological advances comes a thorny decision making responsibility. Christians will not always be satisfied with the advice or explanations of the medical community. Decisions involving medical ethics require prayer and counseling or consultation with those of similar faith.

Abuse Problems

"I hit my father," sobbed Frank.

"I didn't mean to do it. But I'd had it. Yesterday he chased my son with his cane, while cursing and swearing at him. This morning, he left the stove on and burned a pan fast to the burner. This afternoon, he messed himself three times. While I was changing him the third time, my son walked into the room, and Dad yelled at him to get the h_ out of there. I just stood up and slapped his face. His false teeth fell out, and his lip began to bleed. How could I do such a thing?"

Such abuse is mild compared to what one finds in the literature. Abuse not only happens between child and parent, but also in nursing homes by paid staff. Sometimes the abuse is not physical, but rather neglectful. Undoubtedly, the most frightening abuse occurs between child and parent. Adults have a strong sense of "I should be in control of myself," and "He cared for me when I was helpless, how can I do less?" These attitudes, though correct, engender devastating guilt and shame. Such individuals find it most difficult to seek counseling. Yet, this is precisely what they must do.

A counselor could help Frank sort out his situation. While not approving of Frank's action, the counselor can help him see how he has allowed the stress of his circumstances to build beyond his ability to cope. He could then lead Frank through the Scriptures to find forgiveness and help him find alternative methods for controlling himself and his attitudes so that he would be able to manage the stress successfully. The counselor would also help Frank determine alternatives for caring for his father so that he and his wife could have periods of time alone, away from, and with the children. Perhaps the church could also help out. County programs might exist to provide respite care. The counselor could also help Frank sort out his feelings about using these services.

One of my mother's old sayings seems appropriate here. "A stitch in time saves nine." Seeking counsel when the stress of caring has stretched you will save the mending of your self-image, your relationship with God, and your relationship with your elderly parent when the fabric of your self-control begins to tear.

Biblical counseling represents my life work. I have witnessed its value in many arenas. We can greatly ease the problems of aging by the wise use of the resources God has provided for us. Counseling is one of these resources. Draw upon it, do not fear it.

14

LOOKING FORWARD
Trends and Projections

During the last 100 years, society has undergone a phenomenal metamorphosis. Families were once generally large, with four or more children. Grandparents, parents, and their children often lived in the same home, or within close distances. The average life expectancy was less than 60 years of age. When illness common to the elderly struck, death frequently occurred. Nursing homes were not very comfortable, not very accommodating, and not very popular. Very old people also represented a rare phenomenon.

Now, in modern times, high technology health care is available for average Americans. Debilitating illnesses often become a manageable part of life. We currently expect people to live an average of 75 years. Families typically live separated by great distances, often resulting in children who hardly even know their grandparents. Elderly people often live alone, with little or no family support. Nursing homes across America are filled to capacity.

Change will continue. The complexion of our society is expected to continue to change in the years to come. Trends that began earlier in this century have now taken deep root. This chapter attempts to address those very trends that are beginning to cause public officials, social service experts, and economic analysts to begin to look for ways to adapt current programs to handle the future. We took all statistics from the 1991 edition of ***Aging America***, a joint publication sponsored by the Special Committee on Aging, Administration on Aging, Federal Council on Aging, and the American Association of Retired Persons.[12]

Aging America presents data based on Census Bureau

statistics. The Census Bureau bases its estimates on three different sets of assumptions about the course of future mortality in making population projections. These differing assumptions produce a lower, middle, and higher range of figures predicting the trends expected in society. *Aging America* utilizes the midrange set of figures.

The American Population

In 1900, 4% of the population was aged 65 or older. Young people, those under the age of 18, made up about 40 percent of the population.

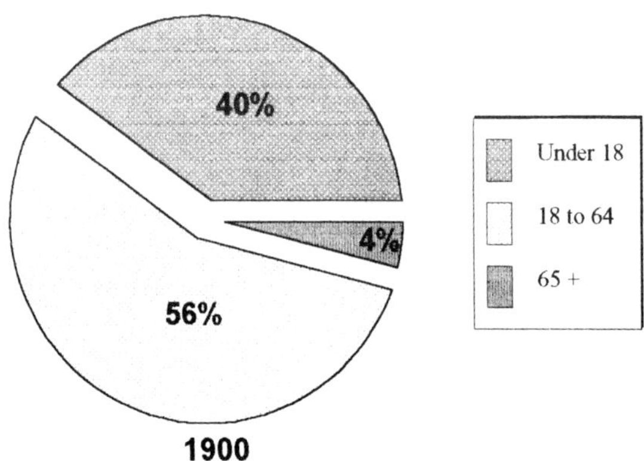

In 1980, only 80 years later, the elderly comprised 11% of the population, while young people had declined to 28%.

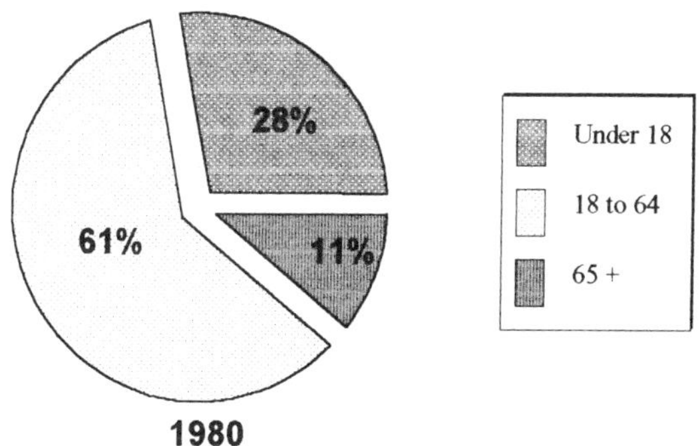

The Census Bureau estimates that, in the year 2030, we will probably have more elderly people 65 or older than people younger than 18 years of age.

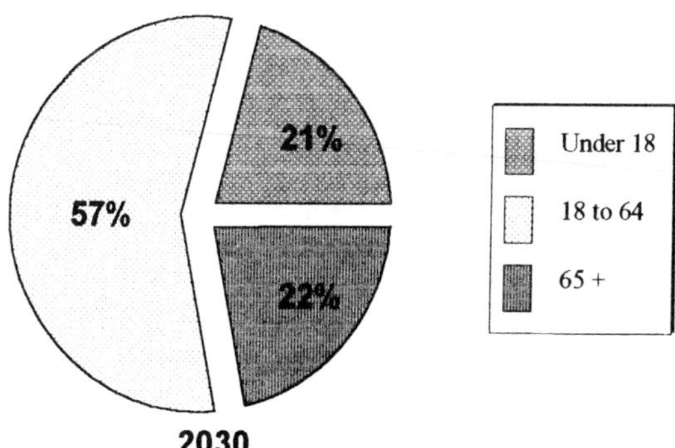

We must look at these numbers in two different ways. First, the percentage of working people to the elderly was once quite high. For every elderly person eligible for Social Security in 1980, nearly six working adults presumably paid into the social service system. However, in 2030, we will only have slightly over two working adults paying into the system for every individual in the older category.

In the year 2030, only one in six Americans will be considered young, or under the age of 18. As this group ages and moves into the category of working-aged adults, and as the large number of working-aged adults moves into the older category, the percentage of working people to elderly people will decline even more. Possibly, beyond 2050, one working adult will be paying into the system to support more than one elderly person.

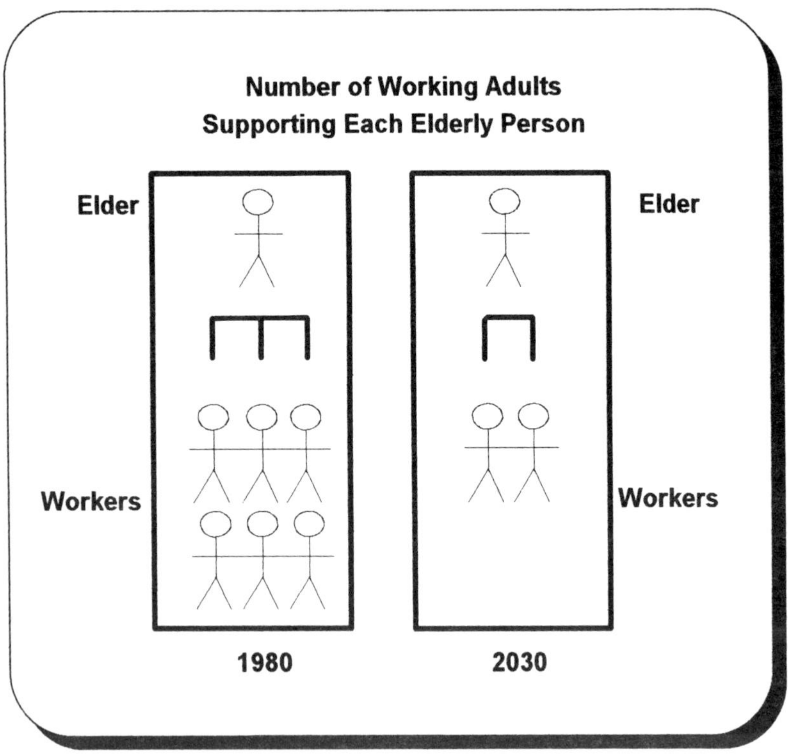

As you can see from the simple charts above, a trend of this kind could indicate that a smaller percentage of workers will carry an increasing burden for generating taxes. The need for monies to be paid into social programs designed to benefit the elderly will become greater with each passing year as the population ages.

A second way to view these figures is by concentrating on the sheer magnitude of people these percentages represent. In 1900, although elderly individuals comprised about 4% of the population, the total population was only about 76 million. In 1980, there were about 227 million people. In 2030, we expect the population to climb to 301 million people. This means that we will have approximately 65 million people aged 65 or older in the year 2030, rising from 26 million in 1980. In 50 short years, the number of elderly people will have more than doubled.

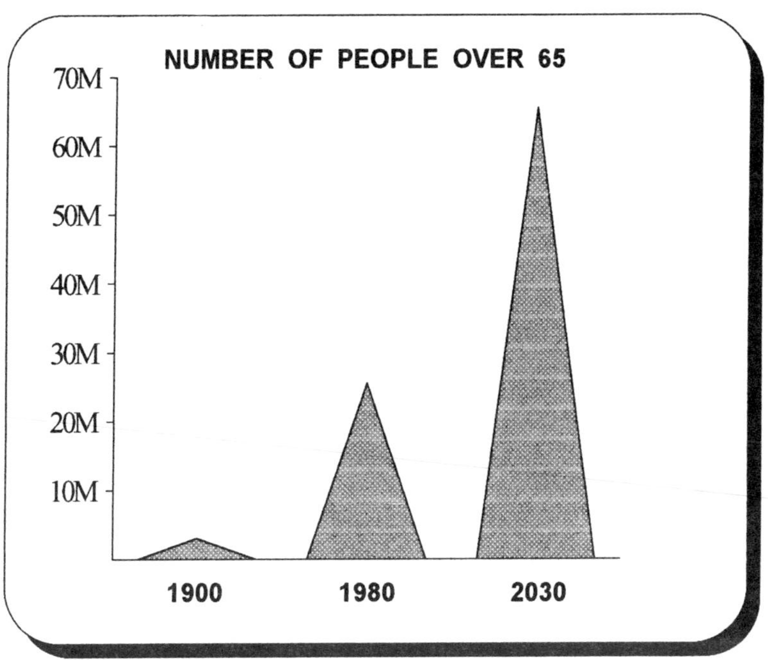

We must also note that there will be a declining percentage of children being born because the percentage of working aged adults is declining. The number of people under age 18 in 1980 was about 63 million. In 2030, the number of people under age 18 is expected to be about the same. In practical terms, this means that working-aged adults will be expected to contribute a larger portion of their incomes to the care of older adults. Some of this additional contribution will be voluntary, and, no doubt, a greater portion will be through taxation. While desiring to look objectively at the Census Bureau projections, the facts seem grim to a society that already struggles with caring for the elderly.

The amount of monies needed to fund health services and retirement incomes will also increase sharply. The increased need for additional people and monies to administer these programs will also add to the strain on America's pocketbook. The health industry will need to grow proportionately to keep up with the additional demands of an ever-increasing population in which the elderly are the fastest growing segment of the population. The need for and use of nursing homes will also increase.

The Census Bureau repeatedly stresses that our nation faces important decisions about the care of the elderly. In 1990, next to China with 63.4 million elderly, the United States has the greatest number of elderly citizens, about 31.6 million. Only 12 other countries have more than 5 million people 65 years of age or older. As the sheer number of elderly people increases, and as the proportion of working adults to elderly adults declines, the needs of this nation and its families will increase in the years to come.

15

SETTING UP YOUR OWN IN-HOME ELDERLY CARE CENTER

The Benefits of In-Home Care

Some Things Money Can't Buy . . .

Although it is true that bringing an elderly relative into your home will also bring in added pressures, stresses, and difficulties, you also face a great potential for a positive impact. An elder can provide a great source of companionship, for both the caregiver, the spouse, and the children. Quite frequently, bringing an additional person into the home will bring about a greater need for, and opportunities for, family interactions with other relatives and friends who would desire to visit with the older relative. But, most of all, the peace of mind that comes from knowing that your older relative is being taken care of will remove the gnawing anxiety that comes from a situation where an older person has needs that he or she cannot meet otherwise.

Some Things There Isn't Enough Money to Buy . . .

People often utilize nursing home care too soon, before the older individual truly requires that level of care. Nursing homes usually cost more than $30,000 per year. Medicare and Medicaid will normally only cover a portion of the cost. Furthermore, stringent requirements for eligibility usually do not allow for the recipient to retain the "inheritance" he or she wishes to pass on to family and friends. However, many of the services offered in a nursing home, for a sometimes substantial daily fee, can be provided in the relative's home with little additional cost. Meals, utilities, and laundry expenses will probably not increase a great deal when an elderly relative enters a family's home. You can usually manage the supervision of medications and coordination of medical treatments as well. When the family does not have the necessary funds to pay for expensive custodial care of an elder relative, in-home care might end up as the only option available to consider.

The Respite Care Crisis

Many individuals who take an older relative into their home to provide the required supervised care find themselves in a most unexpected and difficult situation. Other family members may not want to assist in the elder's care or cannot devote the time and energy needed to give the primary caregiver a much needed rest from his or her ever-present duties. Couples often find it next to impossible to plan a weekend alone together, much less a family vacation with their children. The cost of hiring respite care is often limited by the average American's budget.

Gratefully, this under recognized problem has received the attention of many gifted, creative, and ingenious people in our society. "Time Dollars" represents a new concept introduced in many states. Volunteer organizations, sponsored through churches, community centers, and philanthropic organizations have organized efforts to assist the elderly and disabled in society, without depending primarily on governmental financial aid. Since programs change so rapidly, and eligibility requirements differ from program to program, many people realize that the only help that we may receive comes from the help that we give to one another.

The concept of "Time Dollars" is very simple, yet it requires some initial investment in computers or other tracking aids. Volunteers, usually over the age of 60, offer their time and energy to assist others with various needs. For every hour these volunteers work, they are given a credit to their account. Each credit allows them to "purchase" assistance when they reach a point where assistance becomes necessary. For instance, 62-year-old Ethel works for three hours every week doing laundry and changing linens for John, a 70-year-old man registered with the volunteer organization. John is recovering from cataract surgery and cannot perform many of his regular duties. After John has been certified as capable of performing his normal duties, Ethel then is matched with another individual who has home care needs. Ethel is credited with the hours she works at John's home, and with any other hours she works for other individuals registered with the agency. Over a period of four years, Ethel "bank rolls" a considerable positive balance in her account. One day, should Ethel slip in her driveway on a patch of ice and break her hip, she can begin to "cash in" her volunteer hours by utilizing other volunteers to do her grocery shopping, mow her grass, and drive her to physical therapy appointments.

The concept of "Time Dollars" provides just one of the many ways that people have begun to address the needs of the elderly in positive and dignified ways. Families can also trade time with other families in order to meet their needs for respite care. Especially as our population grows with increasing numbers of people in the elderly category, we must choose to help one another.

Considerations for Your In-Home Elder Care Plan

Safety Features for the Home

In order to determine potential danger areas for your older relative in your home, you first need to determine the activities that he or she might do. Evaluate his typical day by analyzing his specific activities, such as moving around the house, going to the bathroom, using the kitchen, or going in or out of the house. As you begin to review these activities from the perspective of your older relative, many things that can pose a problem will begin to become apparent.

For instance, your older relative normally gets up in the middle of the night to go to the bathroom. Is sufficient lighting provided to prevent your elder from bumping into sharp furniture? Are all doorways to flights of steps closed securely? Are handrails needed near the toilet to help the elder sit and stand safely? Are light switches in the bathroom easy to see and reach? What if your older relative enjoys preparing his or her own breakfast during the week? Does he or she know how to operate the microwave safely? Do any appliances have frayed cords that could pose a shock hazard? Are all items needed to prepare a meal within reach? Are pot handles tight and secure so that a pot won't spill when it is picked up?

As you begin to make a list of the activities that your older relative does on a daily basis, look for potentially harmful and dangerous scenarios. Discuss these with the elder so that he or she recognizes safety precautions to take. Enlist family members to try to determine ways to improve on the safety of the furnishings and setup of the home.

Space Considerations

Can your home accommodate another adult? Will your older relative bring large pieces of furniture with him or her that you will need to place in your home? Nothing will cause more stress for both the caregiver and the family, as well as for the elderly person joining the family, than cramped living quarters that provide no opportunity for privacy. If space is indeed a problem, and the only reasonable option is for the elder to live with you, then buying a new home that affords more livable space, or building an addition onto the present home, may be required. Converting a garage also often offers a low-cost addition to the home that could provide the needed space.

If having your elder live with you becomes necessary, then plan ahead to work out the finances. The older relative may volunteer to pay for the addition. However, if other living relatives stand to inherit from this individual, it is best, in most cases, to have a family conference so that everyone clearly understands the financial arrangements. Unfortunately, you will not always have harmony concerning the proposals offered. Sometimes, you must make a tough decision that may have lasting negative effects. However, even in such cases, the pre-action family conference offers the opportunity for the least amount of rancor and the most amount of understanding.

Finding an interim living solution for your elder until you can make your home suitable to accommodate him is a good idea to consider in order to prevent unnecessary stress during a time of potentially stressful transition.

Financial Assistance

You are not alone in caring for your older relative. If you have decided to take an older relative into your home, make sure that you include other family members in this decision as well. You may find that a sibling, or another relative, might also desire the opportunity to provide care for your elder. Perhaps this relative would find that offering you financial assistance to care for the elder relative would provide an opportunity for him to honor this elder.

On the other hand, perhaps a situation of sharing the elder would also be appropriate. Six months with you in Maine and six months with your sister in Florida might offer a pleasant alternative for your elderly parent who dislikes intense heat in the summer and intense cold in the winter.

Finally, don't be afraid to ask for financial assistance. If after prayerful consideration other relatives cannot assist you financially, remember that God will provide for you as you seek to do His will.

Why Should I Do In-Home Elder Care?

You shouldn't. The only right reason for providing care for an elderly person in your home is not because you feel you "should," but because you can. Also, the God who sustains and provides has brought an individual to you as well as placed a burden on your heart to serve. You also can offer care to the elderly because our time on this earth is a brief flash, and God has called us to love Him and one another with the time He has given to us. Finally, you can serve the elderly because Christ loved us and gave Himself up for us and because He desires you to do so as well. Jesus said:

"I tell you the truth, anyone who gives you a cup of water in my name because you belong to Christ will certainly not lose his reward." (Mark 9:41)

A Caregiver's Self-Responsibilities

A frequent problem for caregivers is exhaustion. From my observation, people who take in a loved one usually fall into two categories. The first category consists of those individuals who will perpetually feel guilty if they do not take in a loved one. Obviously, these people will also feel guilty if they take any time off from care-giving for any reason. The second category consists of those who become caregivers because they have always tended to care for other people's needs. Individuals with the spiritual gift of hospitality or mercy will fit this profile. Thus, caregivers will do well to reproduce the following affirmations, post them in their bedroom, and review them regularly. This regular ritual, along with a daily prayer for wisdom, will enable them to keep life balanced, and will help them to maintain their own health, while contributing to the health of their elderly relative and entire family.

I have a responsibility . . .

. . . to recognize that my role as a caregiver has been providentially arranged.

. . . to seek prayerfully God's assistance for the task of caregiving.

. . . to provide a sense of dignity for my elderly relative by developing a godly attitude about myself and the task of caregiving.

. . . to take care of myself. This is a God-given responsibility and not a matter of selfishness. Proper care of myself will enable me to take better care of my relative.

. . . to seek help from others even though my charge objects. I am responsible to recognize my own limits of endurance and strength.

. . . to maintain those aspects of my life which do not include my elderly relative in the same manner I would if he/she were healthy.

. . . to acknowledge my feelings, to recognize them as symptoms of fatigue or improper attitudes, and to take actions necessary to appropriately process them.

. . . to reject attempts by my elderly relative to manipulate (consciously or unconsciously) me through guilt, anger, or depression.

. . . to offer consideration, affection, forgiveness, and acceptance to my elderly relative regardless of his/her attitudes.

. . . to accept consideration, affection, forgiveness, and acceptance from my elderly relative and recognize that humility does not mean inability to accept gratitude.

. . . to protect my individuality and to make a life for myself that will sustain me and enable me to sustain other normal family relationships during and beyond the time of caring for my elderly relative.

. . . to seek out resources to aid in the caregiving enterprise, including innovations to assist caregivers.

. . . to seek to share my knowledge and experience with others who may profit from my pilgrimage.[13]

16

CAREGIVER'S DIRECTORY OF RESOURCES

To Help Meet the Needs of the Elderly

We have assembled this directory to help you to "honor thy father and thy mother" by giving you access to various assistance information and programs. The appearance of an organization or information in this directory does not signal the endorsement of these resources in their entirety. You need to be aware that the information in this chapter, specifically eligibility requirements, changes periodically as new legislation passes into law.

Income Needs

First, you must identify sources of income for your elderly relative. The obvious source of government income comes from Social Security. However, you must also evaluate any pension plans, annuities, deferred retirement savings, savings accounts, IRA's, savings bonds, life insurance policies, stocks and certificates, property - residence or other, and any possessions of value. Financial management and legal assistance both become necessary to preserve your older relative's assets as long as possible as well as to set up a plan to distribute income to the individual. For individuals who have little or no assets, you may also want to consider the Supplemental Security Income (SSI) program. The Social Security Office will assist you in determining eligibility for SSI.

Social Security

Created in 1935, the Social Security Administration governs this program, funded by employee and employer taxes. Benefits are paid to workers and their dependent survivors. It is designed to provide a baseline economic security for retired or disabled individuals. While eligibility requirements are complex, a basic test of two questions provides an indicator. Has the worker been employed in a "covered" position? This question may be easy to answer by simply checking to see if any Social Security tax was deducted from the payroll check, or if the individual paid self-employment tax. The second qualifying question is not quite as easy to answer. Has the individual worked long enough to reach vested status? The Social Security Administration office can easily determine if the individual has worked long enough to reach the insured or vested status necessary to quality for benefits.

Social Security is not automatically sent to the retiree. The seeker must fill out an application through his or her local Social Security Administration office. If an individual cannot visit an office, a completed application may be mailed, or a representative can visit his home.

Partial benefits may be drawn at age 62 and full benefits at age 65 for many people. However, others may be eligible for retirement at later ages due to new legislation. Depending upon a person's circumstances, an early retirement may be advantageous. You may want to plan a visit to the local Social Security office to determine the details of an early retirement. In retirement planning, you should plan to approach the Social Security office at least 90 days prior to the retirement date. This will ensure the inception of benefits at the date of retirement. If any questions exist about eligibility, it may be helpful to have a representative accompany the applicant when making application for benefits. A member of the clergy, an attorney, a social worker, a friend, or a relative may serve in this capacity.

Supplemental Security Income (SSI)

SSI is a program of the federal government which provides cash assistance for elderly, blind, and disabled individuals who have meager incomes and few assets. In addition, some states subsidize this federal program and sometimes a state's Welfare Department may administer SSI.

The key word to note here is "supplemental." In other words, this program supplements the individual's income so that the participant receives it in conjunction with Social Security, Medicaid, and possibly food stamps. Three requirements determine eligibility: the individual must be at least 65, blind or disabled, and have benefits below the income guidelines set by Congress. You may apply for SSI through your local Social Security Administration office.

Welfare

Welfare refers to money paid by the state or federal government to people of any age who do not have enough to provide for their essential needs - food, rent, and clothing. Need serves as the basic requirement for receiving welfare. Every county has a Welfare Office, and you can find one in all but the smallest towns. You must apply for benefits at the local office.

Food Stamps

Food stamps represent government provided credit for some food purchases. You must have low income and few resources in order to receive food stamps. If an older person receives welfare, he or she should immediately become certified for food stamp program eligibility as well. The amount of food stamps depends on income and family size.

Veteran's Benefits

If a person is 65 or older and a veteran, encourage that individual to check with the Veterans Administration office for possible benefits. Veterans Administration pensions are intended to assist poverty-stricken veterans aged 65 or older or who have become disabled. These benefits also extend to impoverished surviving dependents.

Health Insurance Needs

Medicaid

Medicaid makes medical insurance available to certain low income individuals or families whose income falls below a certain level set by the government. Even if your income exceeds this limit, it may be possible to use a spend-down method to determine if you are eligible for Medicaid. Spend-down recognizes that people still need medical help, even though they may have income over a certain amount. People must apply to their county or state offices of the Department of Social Services, or to the Division of Family Services. These phone numbers will be in your local telephone book.

Medicare

Medicare offers government provided health insurance for individuals aged 65 or older, or for those who are disabled. Eligibility for Medicare has nothing to do with financial need. The Medicare program is divided into two parts: Part A (hospital insurance) and Part B (supplementary medical services, such as visits to the doctor's office). Part A coverage is automatically available to most Social Security recipients and does not require a premium payment. Even if you are covered by an employer health plan, do not delay enrolling in Part A when you become eligible. Part B, however, offers a voluntary insurance, and does require a monthly premium paid by the recipient.

You may delay enrolling in Medicare Part B, but you should not do so unless you are covered by an employer health plan. If you are not covered by an employer health plan, you should enroll in Part B during your initial enrollment period. The initial enrollment period consists of the seven month period beginning three months before you were first able to get Medicare. If you enroll after your initial enrollment period is over, you must wait for a general enrollment period, have your coverage begin the following July, and you may have to pay higher monthly premiums than you would have paid if you had not delayed enrollment. If you are covered by an employer health plan, you may be able to delay enrollment in Medicare Part B without paying higher premiums and without waiting for a general enrollment period to enroll. Delayed enrollment without penalty or wait may be available if you have been covered by an employer health plan (not a plan for retirees) since you were first able to get Medicare.

To find out more information about Medicare, contact your local Social Security Office. If you have other insurance plans, such as an employer-provided health plan, CHAMPUS, or Medicaid, you will need to request specific information about how these coverages are coordinated, and which insurance plan will pay first in the event of a claim. The Social Security Office also provides this information.

Private Insurance

Private health insurance companies make Medigap insurance available for purchase. This policy is designed to fill in some of the "gaps" in Medicare's coverage when Medicare is the primary payor. Although Medigap insurance is strictly voluntary, application to the insurance company for this type of insurance is not guaranteed unless you apply for it within six months of enrolling in Part B Medicare for the first time after becoming age 65. Within this six-month period, called your Medigap open enrollment period, the law does not permit an insurer to sell you a Medigap policy if it duplicates Medicare or other coverage. Thus, if you have an employer health plan at the time you enroll in Part B, you may be unable to purchase a Medigap policy during the open enrollment period. Therefore, if you want to take advantage of the Medigap open enrollment period, you should consider when it is appropriate to enroll in Part B.

Many companies provide their retirees with medical benefits that coordinate with Medicare when the retiree reaches age 65.

These types of benefits usually fill in some of the gaps that Medicare doesn't cover. If a retiree medical plan is available, you may not need supplemental health insurance. It is wise to thoroughly evaluate the services covered to determine if you need additional supplemental health insurance (Medigap).

Other types of insurance policies are available that pay the policyholder directly a predetermined benefit for hospitalization. These types of policies may help defray the cost of hospitalization and typically do not duplicate Medigap coverage. Make careful examination of these types of policies in order to determine if a true financial benefit exists after paying the extra premiums.

In many communities, older people can join an HMO. Many HMO's have entered into an agreement with Medicare and will provide Medicare-covered services to members who have Medicare coverage. Medicare will pay the HMO a monthly fee, which eliminates almost all out-of-pocket expenses for the older person, except the monthly premium paid for Medicare. Many times, an HMO differs from supplemental health plans by providing preventative health care, such as routine physicals. A "primary care physician," usually an internist, coordinates the older person's health care by making referrals to specialists.

You must consider the advantages and disadvantages to this type of health plan. For an older person on a limited income, the HMO may make it easier to budget medical costs. However, your choices of physicians and hospitals become limited, and older people who travel or live away from home for long periods of time may not be eligible for or benefit significantly by this type of health plan.

Veteran's Benefits

Veterans should contact the Veterans Administration office to investigate those services for which they qualify. The military insurance program, CHAMPUS, is available for veterans who meet eligibility requirements. Other medical programs may be available as well.

Housing Needs

Financial assistance is often available in communities to older people who rent or own a home. Utility companies often offer fuel assistance and other services, so contact each utility to determine those benefits for which your elder relative qualifies.

For home owners, many communities and states offer programs to help elderly people maintain and remain in their homes. You will need to investigate programs available for Property Tax Abatement, Property Tax Deferral Loans, Home Maintenance and Repair Programs, and Home Equity Conversion Plans.

The Home Equity Conversion Plan allows older people to convert their home equity into cash. You may also want to investigate Reverse Mortgages as an option. Usually a reverse mortgage helps an individual remain in his or her home by providing monthly checks to the older person based on the equity of the home. These loans usually become due in five to seven years and are paid off through the sale of the older person's home. A Sale/Leaseback Plan allows the owner to sell his or her home to an investor who then leases it back to the older person for a fixed time or for life. A sales agreement establishes the older seller the lifetime right to occupy the property, and it also specifies the rent schedule. The buyer is responsible for maintenance, repairs, and insurance costs. We strongly advise that you consult an attorney and financial advisor before pursuing any of these housing alternatives.

Many housing options exist for the older individual, yet may require aggressive research in each area. Options vary greatly, depending on the community and state. Pay careful attention when analyzing these available options. For the older person who wishes to remain in his or her home, yet can no longer handle all of the expenses and household tasks, you might consider homesharing as an alternative. A housemate, carefully screened and wisely chosen, can help your older relative do chores, share expenses, and provide transportation in exchange for all or part of the rent.

When your older relative does not own his own home, he may also find congregate housing suitable. Usually, in congregate housing, the older person will have his own bedroom, but share other living areas, such as the bathroom, kitchen, and living room. Social activities, meal preparation, and transportation may all be available as well.

Senior housing is often subsidized on the local, state, or federal level. Rents are based on a percentage of income, but you must meet certain income requirements. The demand is high for senior housing, and often long waiting lists exist. It is usually best to place your older relative's name on the waiting list prior to the actual need.

Rental subsidy programs are similar to senior housing, except that older people usually have more options about where they live. One such program is the "Section 8 Rental Assistance" program, where tenants usually pay no more than 30% of their income. The government pays the remaining balance directly to the landlord. Individuals must apply for this program, and eligibility requirements vary from state to state.

A Continuing Care Retirement Community offers a variety of housing alternatives in one location. For the older person who is independent, separate homes or apartments would be available. As the needs of the older person increase, this type of retirement community offers continuing care by making other housing options available. Most often, meal, homemaker and laundry services, as well as recreation activities are made available. If nursing home care becomes a necessity, many times a nursing facility is also available in the same complex. Normally, private individuals own and operate these retirement communities, so you would need to conduct careful research to determine if the older person could afford such care, as well as enjoy this type of living. You should also make it a point to investigate the background information of the owners and developers to determine if the community has sufficient reserves to keep it solvent. It is also important to determine if the down payment is refundable if the resident moves out, whether any portion of the down payment is refundable to the resident's estate if he or she dies after moving in, what services are included in the monthly fee, and whether or not this fee is set or if it could increase.

For the older person who desires the privacy of living in a separate home, but would still like to be near family, self-contained housing units placed in the backyard of an existing home might be allowed in some areas. Town officials or the local housing authority could inform you about zoning restrictions. In some cases, you might create an apartment in the home that allows the older person to stay near the family while also enjoying his privacy.

A retirement community may be a good choice for older relatives who enjoy fair health and have the resources to purchase their own apartments. While residents usually are responsible for all of their own needs, recreational facilities and other services are usually available for those who live within the retirement community.

Home Health Care Needs

Alternative Services, or home care maintenance services, are designed to assist sick and disabled senior citizens as well as handicapped adults. The costs of institutionalization usually are significantly more expensive than home care services.

Home health services are made available to persons 60 years of age or older, and handicapped adults between the ages of 18 and 59, who meet specific guidelines regarding economic, social, and care needs. These services are paid for by General Revenue, Medicaid, Social Services Block Grants, Older Americans Act, and other sources. Medicare may cover some home health services, but standards are very strict, and you must meet many stringent requirements. To find out if you or somebody you know may qualify for these services, contact your county Division of Aging Office. These services enable many people to remain at home and prevent premature or inappropriate institutionalization. Some of these services are listed below, but many communities offer a wide range of services that may not be listed.

1. **Meals-on-Wheels** - For small donations, you can arrange for hot and nutritious meals to be delivered to your elderly relative once or twice a day, five days a week, in many communities. Usually, home meal delivery programs are available in large communities and are frequently staffed by older volunteers.

2. **Silver Citizen Discount Cards** - Many states offer a Silver Citizen Discount card that helps ease the burden

of rising costs of goods and services for senior citizens living on a fixed or limited income. Usually, this involves a percentage discount or other benefit offered by merchants who have voluntarily agreed to participate in the program. Funding for this program is usually administered by the state's Department of Social Services/Division of Aging. To receive more information about whether this type of program exists in your state and to make application, contact your local Area Agency on Aging.

3. **Respite Care** - Respite care is designed to give the caregiver who provides for an elderly relative in the family home a "rest" or break from the demanding duties of home elder care. Unfortunately, respite care, if it is even covered by Medicaid or Medicare, usually offers such a low benefit that very little "rest" time is paid for.

   Many private companies, as well as hospital outpatient departments, churches, and community centers offer respite care services. Such services are usually expensive, and often have restrictions on the duties a respite caregiver can provide. Medication administration is usually one of the services prohibited by non-nurse caregivers. If the older adult requires medication to be administered, frequently a visiting nurse will also need to be scheduled to come to the home. At this time, with the need for respite care growing rapidly, many individuals have begun to enter into cooperative agreements with other in-home elder care providers.

4. **Adult Day Care** - Many adult day care centers are being created in the community. Private organizations, as well as public organizations, recognize the need for families to place their elderly relatives in well staffed, friendly, safe, and dependable care centers while the family caregiver works or runs errands. Area Agencies on Aging should provide listings of adult day care centers in your community.

5. **Denominational Assistance** - Various religious denominations have a variety of programs available. These may be as simple as two hour respite care to a full housing option. These programs are so varied and ever-changing that we have not tried to present any specifics here. This section is simply intended to alert you to the fact that your denomination may have assistance programs to help you and your family. Make an appointment with your clergyperson and/or contact your denominational headquarters.

6. **Transportation** - Many communities provide adult volunteers who are trained to drive vans or personal cars to assist elderly people with their transportation needs. Trips to the grocery store, shopping mall, physician's offices, and even social functions are usually provided.

7. **Personal Care** - The Personal Care Services Program is provided to eligible Medicaid individuals in their homes, to prevent or delay institutionalization. Personal care services are medically-oriented services, provided in the individual's home, to meet the physical needs of the individual, as prescribed by a physician, in accordance with a personal care plan. Personal Care Services may include:

   a) meal preparation, planning, and cleanup;
   b) shampoo, brush, and comb hair;
   c) brushing of teeth when the recipient is unable to do so;
   d) shaving with an electric or safety razor;
   e) bathing - giving bed baths and assisting with tub baths;
   f) transfer of individual to and from a bed to a chair, wheelchair, or walker;
   g) making beds and changing sheets with the service recipient in or out of bed;
   h) cleaning fingernails and toenails (except for diabetic

individuals);

i) medically-related household tasks such as laundering bed linens or cleaning the bathroom; and

j) assisting with self-administered prescriptions.

To be eligible for the Personal Care Services Program, an individual must be currently eligible for Medicaid and recommended for these services by their attending physician. These elderly people will also require nursing care and will be assessed by the Division of Aging to determine that the available services correspond to the individual's needs. If you are currently receiving public assistance or Medicaid, you must simply contact your local Division of Aging social worker to apply for these benefits. If you are not currently receiving public assistance or Medicaid, you must first contact a Division of Family Services case worker and Division of Aging social worker through your local Department of Social Services Office. If you are housebound or hospitalized, a family member, physician, hospital, or nursing home staff member may apply for you.

APPENDIX A
Organizations That Can Help

Alzheimer's Disease

Families who have loved ones afflicted with Alzheimer's disease may call a toll free number for the Alzheimer's Disease and Related Disorders Association (ADRDA). You can reach them at (800) 621-0379. Within Illinois, call (800) 572-6037. ADRDA has more than 160 chapters and 1,000 support groups nationwide to help caregivers. Local ADRDA chapters can provide advice and assistance on many different topics, including respite care and insurance questions.

American Association of Retired Persons

Few organizations offer a more comprehensive, up-to-date listing of pertinent booklets, brochures, newsletters, magazines, and books as the American Association of Retired Persons (AARP). The AARP is a nonprofit, nonpartisan organization with more than 30 million members aged 50 or over. The AARP came into existence in 1958 by Dr. Ethel Percy Andrus, in an effort to better the lives of older Americans through service, advocacy, education, and volunteer efforts. Membership in this organization is a must. Membership dues are inexpensive. You can obtain more information by writing to: AARP, 601 E. Street NW, Washington, D.C. 20049, or call (202) 434-3525.

To order AARP's video, *Survival Tips for New Caregivers*, call (202) 434-2255. AARP also offers caregiving workshops to community organizations and agencies. For further information, contact the Social Outreach and Support Section of AARP at the above address.

Area Agency on Aging

You can find nearly 700 chapters of the Area Agency on Aging located across the United States. They provide free advice, needs assessments, referrals, and information about such local services as adult day care, respite care, home health aid, transportation and escort services, homemaker and chore services, housing services, and support groups. Your local Area Agency on Aging office should be listed in your phone directory.

For help finding your local Area Agency on Aging office, or many other resources available to you, contact the National Association of Area Agencies on Aging by calling their Eldercare Locator, a nationwide directory assistance service to help caregivers. The Eldercare Locator can be reached at (800) 677-1116, or write to: National Area Agency on Aging, 1112 16th St., NW, Suite 100, Washington, D.C. 20036.

Encyclopedia of Associations

In the reference section of your local library, you will find a reference entitled *The Encyclopedia of Associations*. Every year, a current edition of this work is released. Under the listing of "Aging," you will find many important and valuable addresses and phone numbers for nationwide organizations that can assist you.

Home Care Agencies

The National Association for Home Care is a lobbying group and national clearinghouse of information regarding home care agencies. Many helpful pamphlets are available from this agency. For price lists and more information about services available, you can write to the National Association of Home Care at: 228 7th St. SE, Washington, DC 20003, or call (202) 547-7424.

Housing Options

You can receive a free packet of caregiving brochures and information on housing options for seniors by sending a stamped, self-addressed legal sized envelope to: American Association of Homes and Services for the Aging, 901 E Street N.W., Suite 500, Washington, DC 20004-2037, or call (202) 783-2242.

Incontinence

The Simon Foundation offers free information on incontinence, bladder training, and support groups. You can reach them by calling toll free, (800) 23-SIMON, or write to: P.O. Box 835, Wimette, IL 60091.

Additionally, The Alliance for Aging Research offers free brochures on incontinence and bladder training. Training materials for physicians and medical professionals are also available. Write to the Alliance at: 2021 K St. NW, Suite 305, Washington, DC 20006, or call (202) 293-2856.

Legal Services

The transferring of assets to spouse or children and living trusts are best handled by attorneys familiar with Medicaid rules and regulations. An attorney attempting to help a family with the preservation of their assets may get consulting assistance from the American Bar Association by calling (202) 662-8690, or writing to: ABA Commission on the Legal Problems of the Elderly, American Bar Association, 740 15th St., NW, Washington, DC 20005.

The National Academy of Elder Law Attorneys also serves attorneys by educating them about changes in the laws pertaining to Medicare, Medicaid, wills, trusts and estate planning. They may be reached by writing to: The National Academy of Elder Law Attorneys, 1604 Country Club Road, Tucson, AZ 85716, or by calling (520) 881-4005.

You can reach local lawyers familiar with these issues by checking with an Area Agency on Aging Office in your community or a local legal services office.

National Association of Nouthetic Counselors

To find a family or individual counselor in your area who holds to a high standard of biblical counseling, contact the National Association of Nouthetic Counselors for a referral or a list of qualified counselors. You may write to: NANC at 5526 S.R. 26 East, Lafayette, IN 47905, or call (317) 448-9100.

National Association of Professional Geriatric Care Managers

When your elderly relative lives far away from you, and you need help in determining appropriate services available to help care for him, this professional association publishes a $35 directory of care managers listed by state and qualifications. Managers assess the elderly person's needs and help you plan their care. To receive this information, contact them at: 1604 North Country Club Road, Tucson, AZ 85716, or call (520) 881-8008.

National Council on the Aging

The National Council on the Aging publishes many resources for the caregiver, including the most current and complete national directory of caregiver support groups. You can reach The National Council on the Aging by writing to: 409 3rd St., SW, 2nd Floor, Washington, D.C. 20024 or calling (202) 479-1200.

National Hospice Organization

The National Hospice Organization provides referrals for hospices throughout the United States. They also provide membership to their organization at either the professional or individual level. Information about conferences, as well as a catalog with all available publications and videos, is available upon request by writing to: 1901 N. Moore St., Suite 901, Arlington, VA 22209, or calling (800) 658-8898.

National Institute on Aging

This organization provides an information center for publications and referrals to many organizations. They can be reached by calling (800) 222-2225 or writing: NIA - Information Center, P.O. Box 8057, Gaithersburg, MD 20898-8057.

The National Rehabilitation Information Center

The National Rehabilitation Information Center provides information and fact sheets on research, products and resources related to the needs of people caring for parents with physical limitations. You can reach this organization by calling the following toll free number: (800) 34N-ARIC or (301) 588-9284. You may write to them at: The National Rehabilitation Information Center, 8455 Colesville Road, Suite 935, Silver Spring, MD 20910.

The Older Women's League (OWL)

The Older Women's League provides many services to women as caregivers, as well as being advocates for women in obtaining health care, economic security, appropriate housing and freedom from violence and discrimination. For a packet on information of caregiver resources, send a self-addressed, stamped business sized envelope to: OWL, 666 11th Street NW, Suite 700, Washington,

D.C. 20001 or call (202) 783-6686.

Social Security Programs

To ask questions about any of the Social Security programs available, call the toll free Social Security hotline at (800) 772-1213 between 7 a.m. and 7 p.m. on business days.

APPENDIX B
Recommended Reading

The following books, as well as many other helpful books, can be found in your public library or purchased through a local book store.

The Age Care Source Book: a resource guide for the aging and their families. Jean Crichton, New York: Simon & Schuster, 1987.

This is a fact book covering financial, medical and emotional issues regarding aging.

American Guidance for Seniors. Ken Skala, Falls Church, VA: American Guidance, 1991.

For a complete compilation of information that will help older people and their caregivers navigate through the complicated federal, state or county agencies that offer benefits or services.

Caregiving: Helping an Aging Loved One. Jo Horne, Washington, D.C.: Scott, Foresman, Lifelong Learning Division, 1985.

This book is an all-in-one reference book for caregivers.

Guide to Housing Alternatives for Older Citizens. Margaret Gold, Consumer Reports, 1985.

This book provides in-depth information, health, and financial checklists and a listing of key sources for help in dealing with housing issues for the elderly.

The Home Healthcare Solution: a complete consumer guide. Janet Zhun Nassif, New York: Harper & Row, 1985.

This is a complete consumer care guide with shortcuts, tips, and tax-saving advice.

You, Your Parent, and the Nursing Home: A Family's Guide to Long-Term Care. Nancy Fox, Bend, OR: Geriatric Press; Prometheus Books, 1982.

This book helps relatives to cope with emotional and social pressures and shows them how to channel their energies constructively when torn between their responsibilities as parents, children and community members.

ENDNOTES

[1] The following Scriptures will enhance your understanding: Deuteronomy 3:27; Matthew 25:46; John 3:15, 6:54-58, 10:28, 12:25, 17:2-3; Romans 2:7, 5:21, 6:23; 1Timothy 6:12, 19; Titus 1:2, 3:7; Hebrews 9:12; 1 John 1:2, 2:25, 5:11-12; Jude 21.

[2] I have always found it curious that our American system of government imposes a minimum age requirement for Congress and the Presidency but does not impose educational requirements. The church, however, imposes only educational limitations which may allow for people of young age to hold responsible church offices. Perhaps this somewhat obscure Scriptural reference should precipitate a discussion on the biblical principles regarding the minimum age of an individual seeking ordination.

[3] Jay E. Adams, "Retirement -- A Christian Option?", *Journal of Pastoral Practice*, Vol. IV, October 1983, Christian Counseling and Educational Foundation, Laverock, PA, p. 22.

[4] Jay E. Adams, p. 23.

[5] Help with these projects can be obtained from the Christian Advocate Ministry through the office of Mercy Ministries at the Mission to North America (Presbyterian Church in America).

[6] Simon J. Kistemaker, *New Testament Commentary: James and 1-3 John.* Grand Rapids: Baker Book House, 1986.

[7] James M. Stifler, *The Epistle To The Romans.,* Chicago: Moody Press, 1960.

"There are obligations flowing from the endowments of certain gifts, and other obligations flowing from fraternal relations, obligations of love. The former were discussed in 12:1-8 and the latter in 12:9-21. These are all purely spiritual obligations, having their source in the relations to Christ (the Savior). But the Christian has another relation, a natural relation, having its origin not in Christ (the Savior), but in God (the Creator). The former chapter is spiritual or Christian (redemptive); the one before us is divine (creative). These are clearly distinct. Confusion here makes church and state one and reduces Christianity to sociology. It is easy to distinguish between what is spiritual (redemptive) and what is divine (creative). The Holy Spirit has brought about institutions and relations unknown to nature. The church with its various functions is the sum of these, and they have no existence before Christ came. But there were men and relations long before. God instituted the latter. . . for men. They are divine (creative), but not spiritual (redemptive)"

[8] David Torrance & F. Thomas (Eds.) *Calvin's Commentaries: The Epistles of Paul The Apostle To The Romans and To The Thessalonians.* Ross MacKenzie (Translator). Grand Rapids: Eerdmans, 1979, p. 280.

[9] David Torrance, p. 283.

[10] This may be a nonprofit organization or a division of state government. Some states have a multiple number of Area Agency on Aging offices and some only a few. These agencies contract out many of the services they offer to other nonprofit organizations.

[11] Jay Adams has written what is perhaps the first systematic theology of Christian counseling. Christians should not view counseling as a product of the 19th or 20th centuries. A careful study of the Bible reveals ample evidence that God has addressed the issues of ancient and modern life. Therefore, a study of church history leaves no doubt that Christians have practiced counseling over the centuries. See Jay Adams' work entitled *A Theology of Christian Counseling*, Grand Rapids: Zondervan, 1987.

[12] David Pryor, Joyce T. Berry, William S. Cohen, Ingrid Azvedo, Horace B. Deets. *Aging America: Trends and Projections*, Prepared by the U.S. Senate Special Committee on Aging, the American Association of Retired Persons, the Federal Council on the Aging, and the U.S. Administration on Aging, 1991.

[13] This includes an adaptation, revision, and expansion of "A caregiver's bill of rights." Jo Horne. *Caregiving: Helping an Aging Loved One*, Mount Prospect: Scott Foreman and Co., 1985.

MAIL ORDER PAGE

To order additional copies of *The Christian Handbook on Aging* (regular edition or large print edition), complete the following information:

Ship to: *(please print)*

Name: ____
Address: ____
City, State, Zip: ___________________________________
Day telephone number: (___)_____________________________

____ copies of ***The Christian Handbook on Aging***
@ $12.95 each: $_______

____ copies of ***The Christian Handbook on Aging***
in LARGE PRINT, spiral bound @ $13.00 each: $_______

Sub-total: **$_______**

Alabama state tax @ 5% (sub-total x .05): $_______

Postage and handling @ $2.50 each book: $_______

(For orders of three or more, call or fax for postage and handling charges (205) 245-1488)

TOTAL AMOUNT ENCLOSED: **$_______**

Make checks payable to Growth Advantage Communications

Send this order form, with payment, to:

Growth Advantage Communications
641 Mountain View Lake Road
Sylacauga, AL 35150